Dragon Eggs Series

Workbook for books 1

Notes on the Dragon Eggs Series

The Dragon Eggs Series introduces the vowel sounds and their alternative spellings. It can be used to either introduce or consolidate learning at this level. The Dragon Eggs Series has more text to the page than our Dandelion Readers vowel spellings range and is a useful stepping stone in building up children's reading fluency. The series includes ten books, each with a phonic focus. This workbook, based on the stories, includes a variety of activities that teach and consolidate an understanding of the Phonic Code.

Pronunciation
At the beginning of each book, there is a word list to help the reader learn the alternative spellings of vowel sounds in the English Phonic Code. Pronunciation of some sounds may vary, according to regional accents. The word lists may not always match the pronunciation of the student. This point should be discussed and the lists adapted to the student.

Blending not guessing
Students should be encouraged to blend the sounds into words. If there are spellings they do not know, point to the part of the word that is new and tell them the sound. Then get the student to blend the sounds into the word.

Use precise pronunciation
When blending sounds together, say the consonants without the added 'uh' sound, e.g. 'c' 'a' 't' not 'cuh' 'a' 'tuh'.

Teaching alternative spellings
The English Phonic Code is complex. This series presents five to nine alternative spellings for a vowel sound. The teacher may need to introduce these spellings gradually if the student has difficulty learning all the alternative spellings at a time.

Splitting multisyllabic words
It is important to teach students how to split multisyllabic words to enable them to use successful and independent strategies when reading and spelling long words. This workbook allows the teacher to use any method he/she is teaching the student.

New vocabulary
Each new book offers an opportunity to learn new vocabulary on the 'Vocabulary' page. This page explains the words as they appear in the context of the text.

Reading fluency
Reading fluently is reading in a way that ensures comprehension of a text. To read fluently, the reader needs to read:

1. accurately (otherwise she/he may read words incorrectly);
2. at a suitable pace (too slow and the reader will have difficulty holding all the words in working memory to make meaning of a sentence; too fast and this may affect accuracy and comprehension);
3. with suitable expression (be able to pronounce the words correctly and to use punctuation for intonation).

Phonic sequence in the Dragon Eggs Series:
Books 1-10

Book	Title	Phoneme focus	Spellings
1	Lost in the Waves	'ae'	ay, ai, a, a-e, ea, ey
2	Tree Beast	'ee'	ee, ea, e, y, e-e, ie, ei
3	Frozen Solid	'oe'	ow, oa, o, oe, o-e
4	The Sky Worm	'er'	er, ir, ur, or, ear
5	Lost and Found	'ow' and 'oi'	ow, ou and oy, oi
6	Confusing Routes	'oo'	oo, ue, u-e, ew, ou, u
7	Finding the Light	'ie'	igh, ie, i-e, i, y
8	Falling Waters	'or'	or, ore, a, aw, awe, au, ur, al, ough
9	A Daring Raid	'air'	air, are, ear, ere, eir
10	Breaking the Charm	'ar'	ar, a, al, ear, au

Notes on the Dragon Eggs Series workbook

The Dragon Eggs Series comprises ten books, each introducing a number of alternative spellings for a vowel sound. This workbook that complements the series provides some activities that precede and prepare the reader for reading and some that follow reading the books. The aim is to expose the reader to words in text through multiple opportunities for reading. This repeated practice will help her/him commit the words to long-term memory and develop reading accuracy and speed that will enable reading fluency.

1. Before reading the books, students would benefit from practising word-building, blending, reading and sorting activities. These activities feature at the beginning of every chapter in the workbook. An instruction for each activity in the workbook appears at the bottom of each page.

2. Make sure the reader knows the spellings (graphemes) introduced in each book. These are listed on the 'Reading Practice' page in the book.

3. Discuss any new vocabulary words listed on the 'Vocabulary' page, for example:
   a) Model pronunciation of new words with correct syllable stress.
   b) Explain words by providing example sentences and asking the student to do the same.
   c) Discuss similar words (synonyms) and words with opposite meanings (antonyms).

4. Read the book with the student. If the reader has difficulties, share chapters or pages to relieve the reading strain.

5. Model how to use punctuation and intonation to read with expression (prosody).

6. After reading the book, the student can do the follow-up comprehension and spelling activities in the workbook. The teacher can select from the activities in each chapter to maintain interest and variety.

7. Try to get the reader to read the book more than once, as research shows that repeated reading of the same text helps to develop reading fluency. This can be done by asking the reader to read the book to another person or to read the book a second time, this time with greater expression.

8. Each chapter of the workbook includes games that are great for reinforcement. These can also be photocopied and sent home. It is useful to revisit these as the series progresses to help reinforce learning.

Dragon Eggs Series

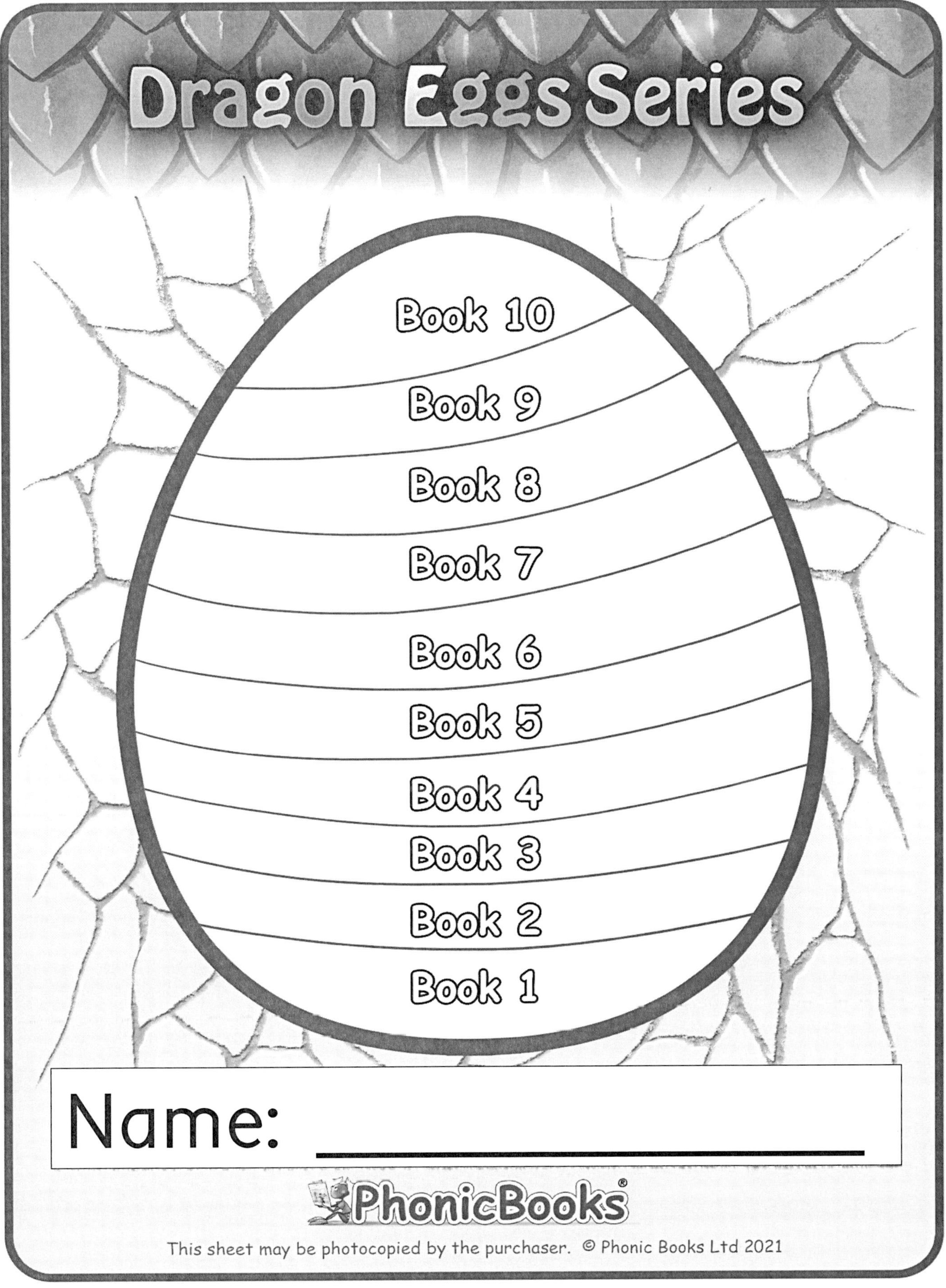

Name:

PhonicBooks®

Students can use this page as a personalised front cover for their Dragon Eggs Series work. They may like to colour each ring of the egg as they read the books in the series.

Book 1: Lost in the Waves
Contents

Book 1: Lost in the Waves

Blending and segmenting: 'ae'

tail	t	ai	l			
they						
mate		a		e		
baby						
great						
drain						
plate						
prey						
spray						
snake						
breaking						
taking						

Blend the sounds into a word. Segment the word into sounds by writing one sound in each square. Split vowel spellings (a–e) are represented by half squares linked together.

Book 1: Lost in the Waves

Reading and sorting words with 'ae' spellings

ai	ay	a-e	a	ea	ey

strain	blame	pray	brain
stain	frame	baby	clay
sale	able	they	faint
great	late	lazy	tray
nail	break	flame	angel
day	pain	steak	mate
David	stay	trail	grey
making	drain	whale	spray

Photocopy this page onto card and cut out the words. Read and sort the cards out according to the 'ae' headings at the top of the page.

Book 1: Lost in the Waves

Reading and spelling words with 'ae' spellings

ai	ay	a–e

a	ea	ey

pale   tail   great   David   May   hate   tray   drain
prey   flame   hay   break   grey   chain   spray   flame
steak   rain   they   table   fail   made   baby   clay

List the words according to the 'ae' spellings.

Book 1: Lost in the Waves

Timed reading of words with 'ae' spellings

<table>
<tr><td>male</td><td>table</td><td>play</td><td>faint</td><td>shame</td><td>late</td><td>paint</td></tr>
<tr><td>tray</td><td>nail</td><td>sacred</td><td>flame</td><td>quaint</td><td>break</td><td>they</td></tr>
<tr><td>day</td><td>pain</td><td>able</td><td>grey</td><td>steak</td><td>mate</td><td>stay</td><td>trail</td></tr>
</table>

1st try	Time:

<table>
<tr><td>male</td><td>table</td><td>play</td><td>faint</td><td>shame</td><td>late</td><td>paint</td></tr>
<tr><td>tray</td><td>nail</td><td>sacred</td><td>flame</td><td>quaint</td><td>break</td><td>they</td></tr>
<tr><td>day</td><td>pain</td><td>able</td><td>grey</td><td>steak</td><td>mate</td><td>stay</td><td>trail</td></tr>
</table>

2nd try	Time:

<table>
<tr><td>male</td><td>table</td><td>play</td><td>faint</td><td>shame</td><td>late</td><td>paint</td></tr>
<tr><td>tray</td><td>nail</td><td>sacred</td><td>flame</td><td>quaint</td><td>break</td><td>they</td></tr>
<tr><td>day</td><td>pain</td><td>able</td><td>grey</td><td>steak</td><td>mate</td><td>stay</td><td>trail</td></tr>
</table>

3rd try	Time:

This timed reading activity is for the student to improve her/his reading speed and fluency. Ask the student to read the words as fast as she/he can. Record the time in the box. Repeat the activity. This sheet can be cut or folded along the dotted lines to allow for different presentations.

Book 1: Lost in the Waves

Chunking two-syllable words with 'ae' spellings

Word	Syllable 1	Syllable 2	Whole word
gatecrash	gate	crash	gatecrash
haystack			
payment			
complain			
breaking			
table			
blameless			
railway			
display			
escape			
steakhouse			
afraid			
awake			
making			

Split the word into two syllables. Write each syllable in a box.
Write the whole word while saying the syllables. This worksheet allows the student to use the approach she/he has been taught for splitting words.

Book 1: Lost in the Waves
Syllable game 1

Die 1

Die 2

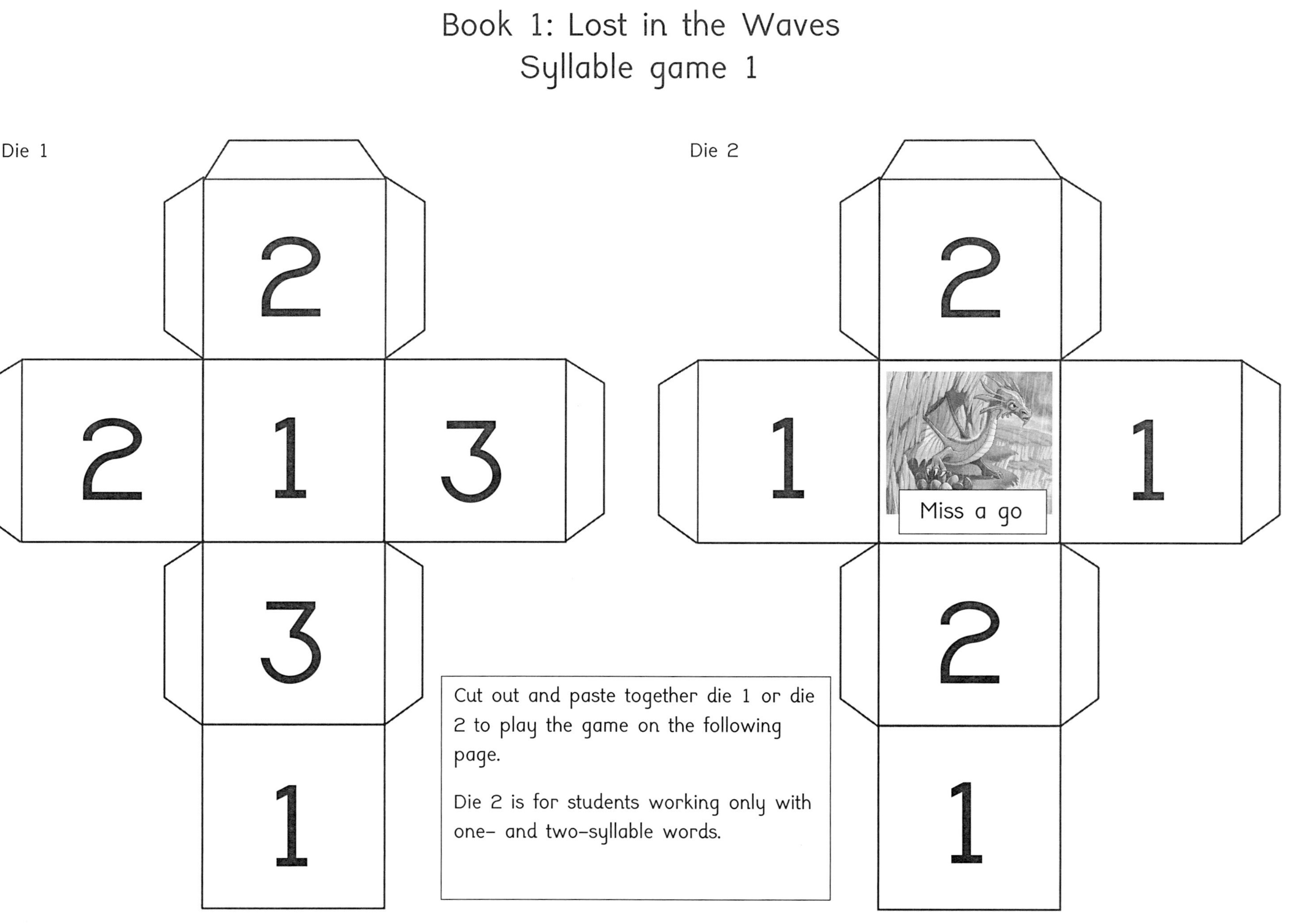

Cut out and paste together die 1 or die 2 to play the game on the following page.

Die 2 is for students working only with one- and two-syllable words.

Book 1: Lost in the Waves

Syllable game 2

game	fainted	calculate
stay	playful	estimate
train	raindrops	emigrate
great	breaking	hesitate
shape	baby	betrayal
they	obey	conveying

A game for 2 to 4 players

Photocopy this page onto card and cut the words out. Write the number of syllables in each word on the back of each card. For ease, the words have been arranged here in columns of one-, two- and three-syllable words. Use only the first two columns of cards for students working with just one-and two-syllable words. Turn the cards word-side up and mix up on a table.

Players take it in turns to roll the die and find a word that has the corresponding number of syllables. The player turns over the card they have selected to check they are right. If they are right, they keep the card. If not, the card is turned over again and remains in play.

Book 1: Lost in the Waves

Phonic patterns

Colour in the words with 'ae' spellings.

hand	frail	great	whale
shame	saddle	jump	black
baking	rattle	they	chain
landing	spray	explain	band
display	steak	able	relay

Fold this sheet along the dotted line. Read the words in the column on the left. Listen to the sounds in the words. Colour in the boxes with words that have 'ae' spellings. Repeat this with the other columns. Unfold the sheet and check that the correct words have been coloured in. This sheet may be photocopied by the purchaser. © Phonic Books Ltd 2021

Book 1: Lost in the Waves

Is it true?

Bella, the dragon, is in a cave. It is a very sunny day. Her eggs get lost under a heap of rocks.

Mina is on the beach with her mum.

Mina finds an egg! It belongs to a mother snake. She wants to help get the egg back to its mum.

Mina sets off to try and find the rest of the eggs.

Mina's cart crashes into a pond.

Mina meets a great big animal. He runs away from her.

There are 6 things in the story above that are not true. Can you spot them?

Ask the student to read the text carefully and circle any false information that has been planted in the story.

This sheet can be cut or folded along the dotted line before presenting to the student.

----

6 things that are not true:

It is not a sunny day. The eggs are not lost under a heap of rocks. Mina is not on the beach with her mum. The egg does not belong to a mother snake. The cart does not crash into a pond. The big animal does not run away from her.

This sheet may be photocopied by the purchaser. © Phonic Books Ltd 2021

Book 1: Lost in the Waves

Retelling the story

Use the story cards to sequence and tell the story.
Can be used as either an oral or a written activity. The teacher can choose whether to number any of cards 2 to 6.

Book 1: Lost in the Waves

Picture the scene

Mina is holding an egg.

The big animal is next to her.

There is a wheel from the cart in front of them.

The sun is up.

There is sand under the big animal and Mina.

Ask the student to read the text carefully and draw the details of the picture as described in the text. Remind the student to read all the instructions through once before starting drawing.

Book 1: Lost in the Waves

Dictation

The wind whipped up. Rocks smashed __ __ __ __

and __ __ __ __ __   __ __ __ __ __ __   the

__ __ __ __.

Bella clung to her eggs, but the __ __ __ __ __

were too strong. The __ __ __ __ __   __ __ __ __

swept Bella and the eggs out into the sea. The eggs

were snatched __ __ __   by the __ __ __ __ __!

Use the text at the bottom of the page for dictation. The section for dictation can either be cut off by the teacher or be folded along the dotted line to allow the student to self–check their spellings on completion. Dictate the passage to the student. Ask her/him to spell the missing words, writing a sound on each line. Explain that longer lines indicate spellings with more than one letter, e.g. r ai n.

The wind whipped up. Rocks smashed **a g ai n** and **a g ai n** **a g ai n s t** the **c a v e**.

Bella clung to her eggs, but the **w a v e s** were too strong. The **c r a z y** **g a l e**

swept Bella and the eggs out into the sea. The eggs were snatched **a w ay** by the

w a v e s!

Book 1: Lost in the Waves

Developing vocabulary: **gazed**

The word 'gazed' is used here in Book 1:

'gazed' means: looked at with great interest

Circle the word or phrase that could be replaced with the word 'gazed' in the following text:

The cakes were fresh and were filled with thick red jam. I looked at them longingly as Mum put them on the table.

Can you write two different sentences of your own using the word 'gazed'?

1.

____

____

2.

____

____

Book 1: Lost in the Waves

Reading fluency

It was a wet day on the cliffs. Bella, the dragon, hid in her damp cave. She cradled her frail eggs against the rain and the gales of wind.

"My babies are not safe!" she wept.

The wind whipped up. Rocks smashed again and again against the cave. Bella clung to her eggs, but the waves were too strong. The crazy gale swept Bella and the eggs into the sea. The eggs were snatched away by the waves!

Next day, the rain and gales had stopped. Mina skipped along the sand, picking up odds and ends that had been swept in by the waves. She spotted an odd shape, hidden in the damp sand.

"Dad," she yelled. "I think it's an egg!"

Ask the student to read through the passage to familiarise themselves with the text.
Read it through for them again to model reading with expression and attention to punctuation.
Ask the student to read the passage again, thinking about adding expression to their reading and following punctuation in the passage. Students who struggle with punctuation may benefit from highlighting the punctuation in the text before reading.
Teachers can fold the page to cover the bottom paragraph of text to offer a shorter passage if needed.

Book 1: Lost in the Waves

Make a page for a comic – reading comprehension

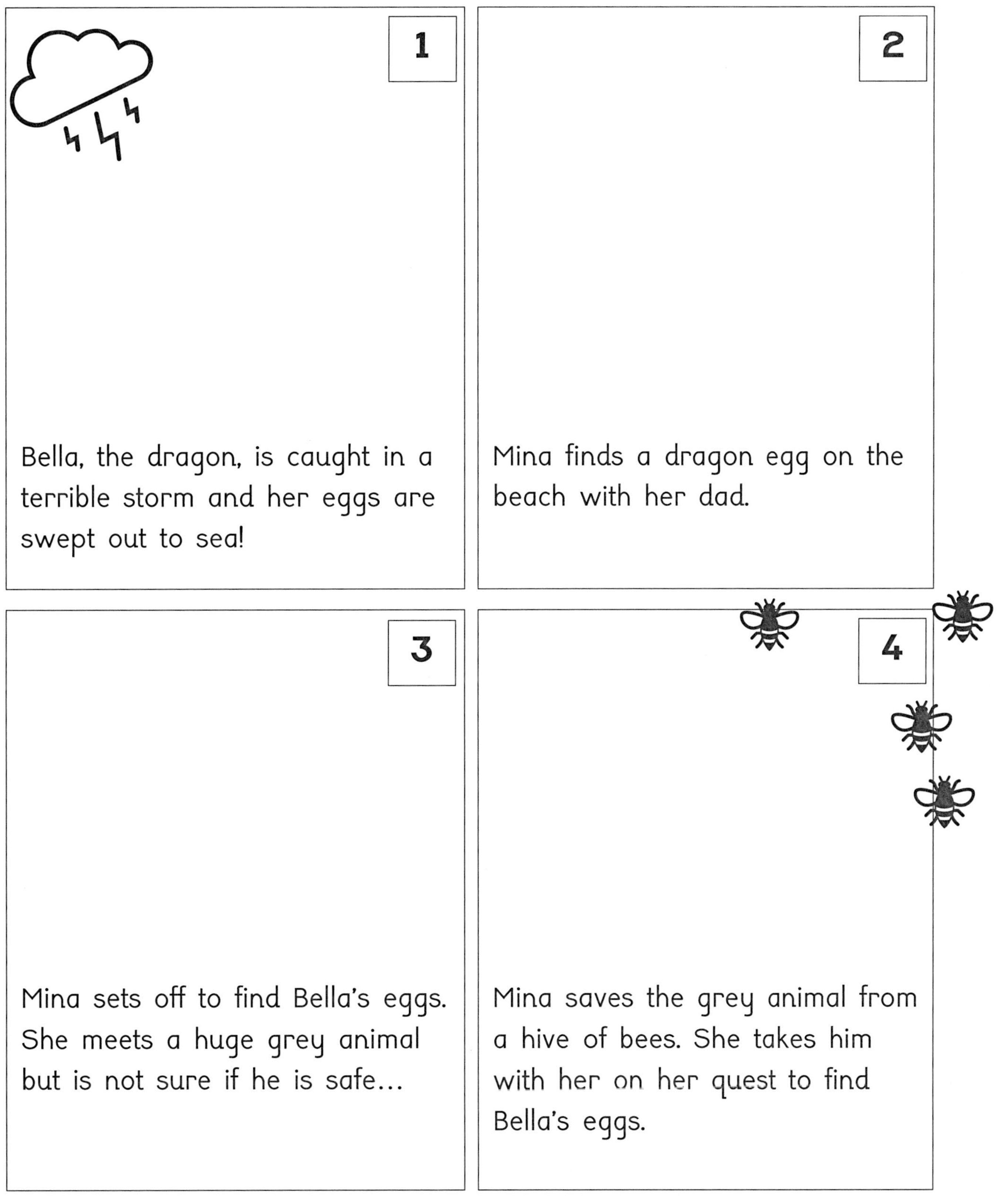

1

Bella, the dragon, is caught in a terrible storm and her eggs are swept out to sea!

2

Mina finds a dragon egg on the beach with her dad.

3

Mina sets off to find Bella's eggs. She meets a huge grey animal but is not sure if he is safe…

4

Mina saves the grey animal from a hive of bees. She takes him with her on her quest to find Bella's eggs.

Ask the student to read the text and draw a picture to match the text in each box.

Book 1: Lost in the Waves

Dice game: words with 'ae' spellings

clay	mate	nail	acorn	tray	great
table	they	late	waist	break	spray
game	tail	cable	cake	David	say
rain	baby	steak	same	aim	able
trail	tape	make	day	blame	wait

This game is for two players. Each player needs a batch of counters of one colour. The players take turns to throw the die. They read a word in the column that corresponds to the number on the die and place their counter on that word. The first to have three of her/his counters in a row in any direction is the winner. This sheet may be photocopied by the purchaser. © Phonic Books Ltd 2021

Book 1: Lost in the Waves   Stepping stones reading game: 'ae' words

A game for 1–4 players: Play with counters and dice.
Players should read aloud the words that they land on at the end of each turn and follow the direction arrows if they land on them.

This sheet may be photocopied by the purchaser. © Phonic Books Ltd 2021

Book 1: Lost in the Waves

Spelling assessment: words with 'ae' spellings

1.

ai	ay	a	a–e	ea	ey
rain	day	baby	name	break	they
faint	play	table	late	steak	prey
brain	spray	bacon	shame	great	grey

2.

ai	ay	a	a–e	ea
sprain	payment	David	gatecrash	breaking
fainted	today	acorn	blameless	steakhouse
explain	haystack	making		

These lists can be used as a spelling assessment at the end of each book. The teacher can add words from list 2 for students who are ready for that stage. When dictating a word, first say the word on its own. Next, say a sentence with the word in it (to put the word in the context of a sentence) and then repeat the word. This ensures that the student has understood the word correctly, e.g. "Fainted. The boy fainted when he saw the mouse. Fainted."

Book 2: Tree Beast
Contents

Book 2: Tree Beast

Blending and segmenting: 'ee'

seem	s	ee	m			
each						
theme		e		e		
me						
grief						
sunny						
delete						
sheep						
cream						
field						
began						
scream						

Blend the sounds into a word. Segment the word into sounds by writing one sound in each square.
Split vowel spellings (e–e) are represented by half squares linked together.

Book 2: Tree Beast

Reading and sorting words with 'ee' spellings

ee	ea	e	ie	ei	e-e	y

feel	steal	reach	thief
compete	shriek	begin	teach
reed	sunny	tree	speak
seem	messy	see	peep
she	creep	sweet	leak
field	sneak	cream	sheet
seize	belong	dream	green
Pete	relax	be	happy

Photocopy this page onto card and cut out the words. Read and sort the cards out according to the 'ee' headings at the top of the page.

Book 2: Tree Beast

Reading and spelling words with 'ee' spellings

ee

ea

e-e

ie

y

e

ei

tree   ceiling   sunny   peach   speak   she   theme   see
chilly   these   feel   field   cream   shriek   me   complete
dream   wheel   seize   happy   treat   street   we

List the words according to the 'ee' spellings.

Book 2: Tree Beast

Timed reading of words with 'ee' spellings

treat　keep　me　cream　funny　please　field
seize　be　speed　dream　freedom　real
grumpy　he　sunny　feet　squeeze　thief　we
believe　read

1st try　　**Time:**

---

treat　keep　me　cream　funny　please　field
seize　be　speed　dream　freedom　real
grumpy　he　sunny　feet　squeeze　thief　we
believe　read

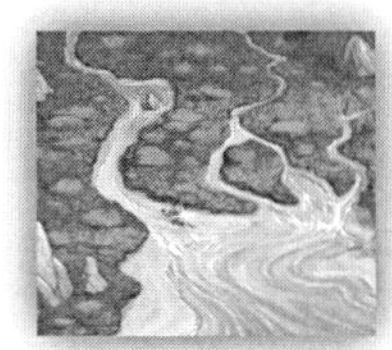

2nd try　　**Time:**

---

treat　keep　me　cream　funny　please　field
seize　be　speed　dream　freedom　real
grumpy　he　sunny　feet　squeeze　thief　we
believe　read

3rd try　　**Time:**

This timed reading activity is for the student to improve her/his reading speed and fluency. Ask the student to read the words as fast as she/he can. Record the time in the box. Repeat the activity. This sheet can be cut or folded along the dotted lines to allow for different presentations.

Book 2: Tree Beast

Chunking two-syllable words with 'ee' spellings

evil	e	vil	evil
freezing			
weaken			
complete			
belief			
creeping			
easy			
achieve			
greedy			
speaking			
seeded			
deeper			
beetle			
heater			

Split the word into two syllables. Write each syllable in a box.
Write the whole word while saying the syllables. This worksheet allows the student to use the approach she/he has been taught for splitting words.

Book 2: Tree Beast
Syllable game 1

Die 1

Die 2

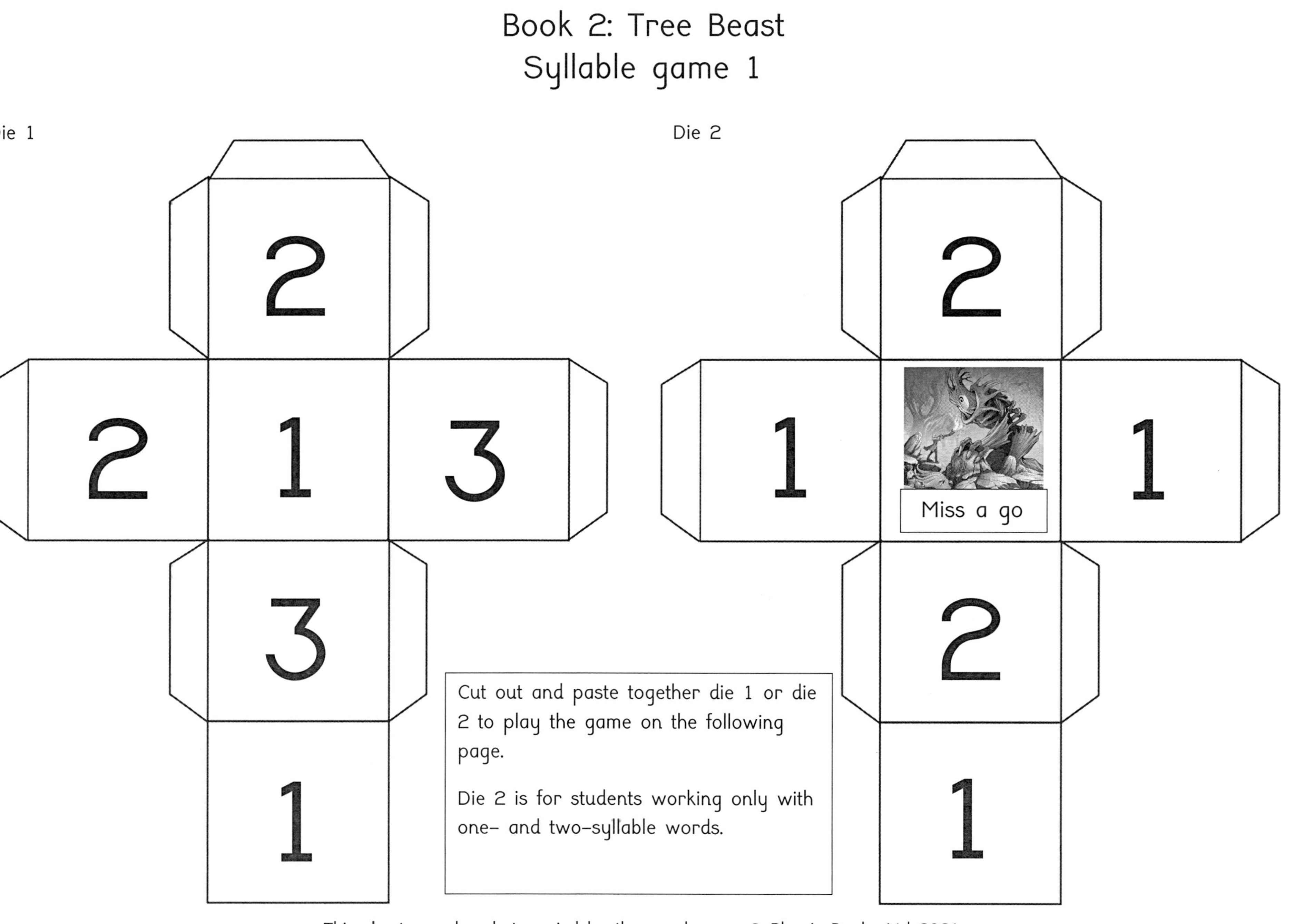

Cut out and paste together die 1 or die 2 to play the game on the following page.

Die 2 is for students working only with one- and two-syllable words.

Book 2: Tree Beast

Syllable game 2

treat	grumpy	beekeeper
cream	feeling	completely
squeak	reading	believing
free	treetop	peacefully
sleep	between	Japanese
she	twenty	family

A game for 2 to 4 players

Photocopy this page onto card and cut the words out. Write the number of syllables in each word on the back of each card. For ease, the words have been arranged here in columns of one-, two- and three-syllable words. Use only the first two columns of cards for students working with just one- and two-syllable words. Turn the cards word-side up and mix up on a table.

Players take it in turns to roll the die and find a word that has the corresponding number of syllables. The player turns over the card they have selected to check they are right. If they are right, they keep the card. If not, the card is turned over again and remains in play.

Book 2: Tree Beast

Phonic patterns

Colour in the words with 'ee' spellings.

happy	swept	metal	week
yellow	speech	freedom	blend
thief	rattle	treat	me
left	please	explain	band
agree	beds	theme	messy

Fold this sheet along the dotted line. Read the words in the column on the left. Listen to the sounds in the words. Colour in the boxes with words that have 'ee' spellings. Repeat this with the other columns. Unfold the sheet and check that the correct words have been coloured in.

Book 2: Tree Beast

Is it true?

There are 7 things in the story above that are not true. Can you spot them?

Ask the student to read the text carefully and circle any false information that has been planted in the story.

This sheet can be cut or folded along the dotted line before presenting to the student.

----

7 things that are not true:

The big animal does not tell Mina his name is Bain. Mina does not have a bag of seeds in her bag. Mina does not follow some monkeys into the trees. The green egg is not in a stream. Pete does not swing in the trees. The monster does not trip and drop the egg. Pete does not make the tree monster feel sleepy by singing to him.

Book 2: Tree Beast

Retelling the story

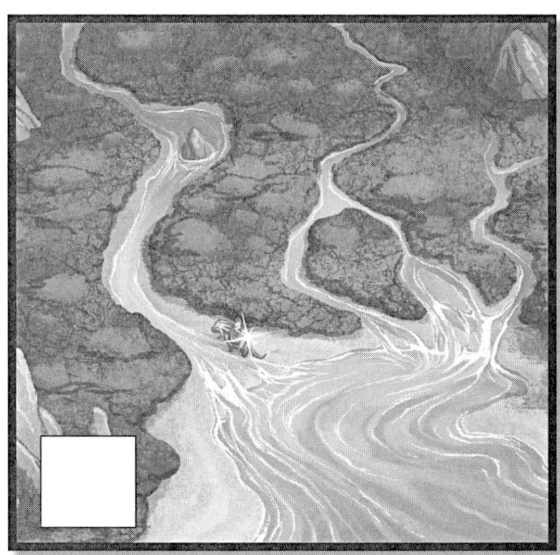

Use the story cards to sequence and tell the story.
Can be used as either an oral or a written activity. The teacher can choose whether to number any of cards 2 to 6.

Book 2: Tree Beast

Picture the scene

The tree monster is in the middle of the picture.

He is holding an egg in his hand.

Mina is in front of the tree monster.

There is a path under the tree monster.

There are three trees in the picture.

Ask the student to read the text carefully and draw the details of the picture as described in the text. Remind the student to read all the instructions through once before starting drawing.

Book 2: Tree Beast

Dictation

It was a   __ __ ___   __ ___ __ __. Mina felt   __ ___ __
at the   ___ ___ __!

"__ ___ __   that egg!"   __ __ __ ___ __ ___   Mina.

The   __ __ ___ __ __   __ __ __   __ ___ __ ___

__ ___ __ ___ __   for her. It grabbed Mina and

__ ___ ___ __ ___   her, lifting her off her feet.

"Bain!" she yelled. "Help   __ __! I   __ ___ __   you."

Use the text at the bottom of the page for dictation. The section for dictation can either be cut off by the teacher or be folded along the dotted line to allow the student to self-check their spellings on completion. Dictate the passage to the student. Ask her/him to spell the missing words, writing a sound on each line. Explain that longer lines indicate spellings with more than one letter, e.g. t r ee.

It was a **t r ee** **b ea s t**. Mina felt **w ea k** at the **kn ee s**!

"**L ea ve** that egg!" **s c r ea m ed** Mina.

The **c r ee p y** **t r ee** **b ea s t** **r ea ch ed** for her. It grabbed Mina and **s qu ee z ed**

her, lifting her off her **f ee t**.

"Bain!" she yelled. "Help **m e**! I **n ee d** you."

Book 2: Tree Beast

Developing vocabulary: **keen**

The word 'keen' is used here in Book 2:

'keen' means: to be enthusastic about and like something

Circle the word or phrase that could be replaced with the word 'keen' in the following text:

It had been a long, rainy day. When the sun came out, Jake was really happy to be able to go out on his bike again.

Can you write two different sentences of your own using the word 'keen'?

1.

____

____

2.

____

____

Book 2: Tree Beast

Reading fluency

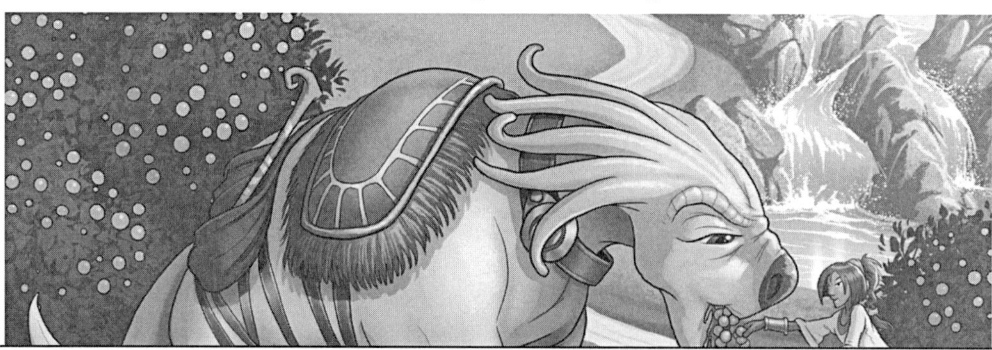

The big animal seemed happy to be with Mina. She made him a
saddle with cloth from the trailer.

"I can't keep thinking of you as just a beast," Mina told him. "You
need a name. I think Bain is a good, strong name."

Bain grinned. He seemed keen on his name!

Suddenly Bain's tummy rumbled! He was hungry!

"We need to eat," agreed Mina. "A handful of berries from these
trees will keep us going."

Bain grinned as he munched the sweet berries. What a feast!

They set off along a sandy beach.

"We can't stop yet," Mina mumbled sleepily. "We need to keep
seeking out the eggs."

Bain seemed to be grinning at her. He was offering her a lift!

Mina quickly hopped up on his back.

Ask the student to read through the passage to familiarise themselves with the text.
Read it through for them again to model reading with expression and attention to punctuation.
Ask the student to read the passage again, thinking about adding expression to their reading and following
punctuation in the passage. Students who struggle with punctuation may benefit from highlighting the
punctuation in the text before reading.
Teachers can fold the page to cover the bottom paragraph of text to offer a shorter passage if needed.

Book 2: Tree Beast

Make a page for a comic – reading comprehension

<table>
<tr><td>

1

Mina names the big animal Bain. Mina and Bain eat a meal of sweet berries.

</td><td>

2

Mina sets off to find the dragon eggs. She finds a green egg. A tree monster has it in his hand!

</td></tr>
<tr><td>

3

The tree monster is asleep. Pete helps Mina swing over the tree monster on a rope to get the green egg.

</td><td>

4

Pete blows his horn which makes the tree monster feel sleepy and peaceful. Mina and the green egg are safe.

</td></tr>
</table>

Ask the student to read the text and draw a picture to match the text in each box.

Book 2: Tree Beast

Dice game: words with 'ee' spellings

1	2	3	4	5	6
real	steam	belong	theme	free	cream
me	creep	steep	happy	messy	funny
keep	shield	seize	field	dream	he
chief	street	relax	reef	speak	bee
leaf	each	deep	please	wheat	these

This game is for two players. Each player needs a batch of counters of one colour. The players take turns to throw the die. They read a word in the column that corresponds to the number on the die and place their counter on that word. The first to have three of her/his counters in a row in any direction is the winner. This sheet may be photocopied by the purchaser. © Phonic Books Ltd 2021

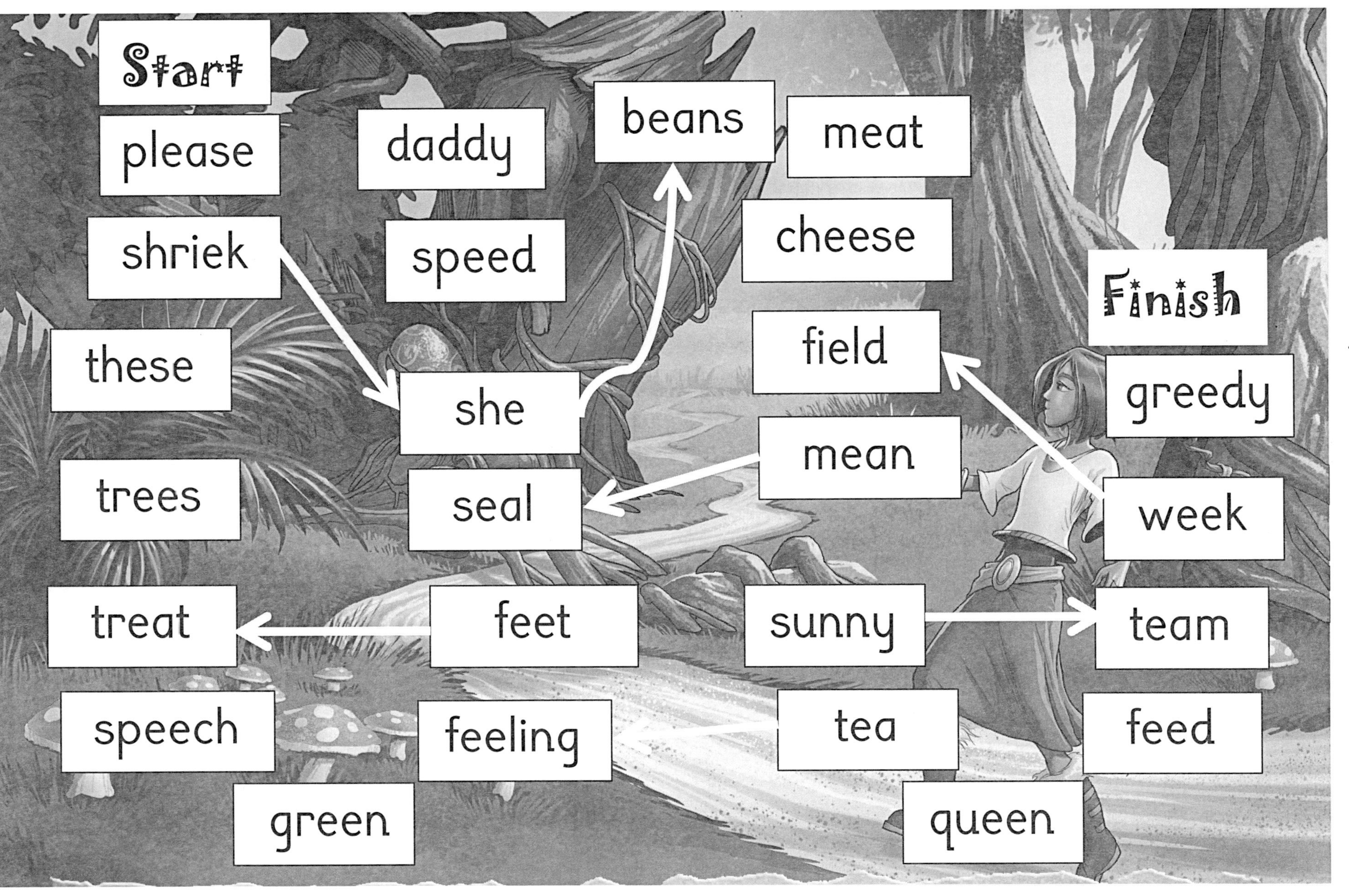

A game for 1–4 players: Play with counters and dice.
Players should read aloud the words that they land on at the end of each turn and follow the direction arrows if they land on them.

This sheet may be photocopied by the purchaser. © Phonic Books Ltd 2021

Book 2: Tree Beast

Spelling assessment: words with 'ee' spellings

1.

ee	ea	e	e-e	y	ei	ie
bee	sea	he	Pete	sunny	seize	thief
week	meal	she	theme	happy		chief
freed	speak	evil	these	floppy		shield

2.

ee	ea	e	e-e	y	ei	ie
greens	dreams	relax	compete	sadly	ceiling	priest
agree	bleach	begin	athlete	angry	receive	piece
screech	scream	belong	complete	hungry		shriek

These lists can be used as a spelling assessment at the end of each book. The teacher can add words from list 2 for students who are ready for that stage. When dictating a word, first say the word on its own. Next, say a sentence with the word in it (to put the word in the context of a sentence) and then repeat the word. This ensures that the student has understood the word correctly, e.g. "Angry. The girl was angry when the bus was late. Angry."

Book 3: Frozen Solid
Contents

Book 3: Frozen Solid

Blending and segmenting: 'oe'

go

toe

hope

low

groan

snows

stone

boat

grow

joking

flowing

roast

Blend the sounds into a word. Segment the word into sounds by writing one sound in each square.
Split vowel spellings (o–e) are represented by half squares linked together.

Book 3: Frozen Solid

Reading and sorting words with 'oe' spellings

o	oa	ow	o-e	oe

know	soap	Rome	hero
alone	toast	crow	close
boast	show	goat	note
toe	so	bone	coat
rope	go	hole	bow
joke	most	pole	flow
groan	post	float	goes
moan	roll	throw	toe

Photocopy this page onto card and cut out the words. Read and sort the cards out according to the 'oe' headings at the top of the page.

Book 3: Frozen Solid

Reading and spelling words with 'oe' spellings

ow	oa	o-e
___________	___________	___________
___________	___________	___________
___________	___________	___________
___________	___________	___________
___________	___________	___________

o	oe
___________	___________
___________	___________
___________	___________

roast hope road blow groan show joke no

throat foe grow bone bloat go drove toe

throw spoke so snow woe

List the words according to the 'oe' spellings.

Book 3: Frozen Solid

Timed reading of words with 'oe' spellings

coat	mole	crow	moan	slope	goat	no	bloat
roll	moat	slow	pole	toad	spoke	grow	so
home	boat	show	toast	go	toes	low	

1st try   Time:

---

coat	mole	crow	moan	slope	goat	no	bloat
roll	moat	slow	pole	toad	spoke	grow	so
home	boat	show	toast	go	toes	low	

2nd try   Time:

---

coat	mole	crow	moan	slope	goat	no	bloat
roll	moat	slow	pole	toad	spoke	grow	so
home	boat	show	toast	go	toes	low	

3rd try   Time:

This timed reading activity is for the student to improve her/his reading speed and fluency. Ask the student to read the words as fast as she/he can. Record the time in the box. Repeat the activity. This sheet can be cut or folded along the dotted lines to allow for different presentations.

Book 3: Frozen Solid

Chunking two-syllable words with 'oe' spellings

hopeless	hope	less	hopeless
moaning			
boastful			
tiptoes			
hollow			
homeless			
broken			
oboe			
lonely			
woeful			
posting			
toaster			
roasted			
open			

Split the word into two syllables. Write each syllable in a box.
Write the whole word while saying the syllables. This worksheet allows the student to use the approach she/he has been taught for splitting 'words.

Book 3: Frozen Solid
Syllable game 1

Die 1

Die 2

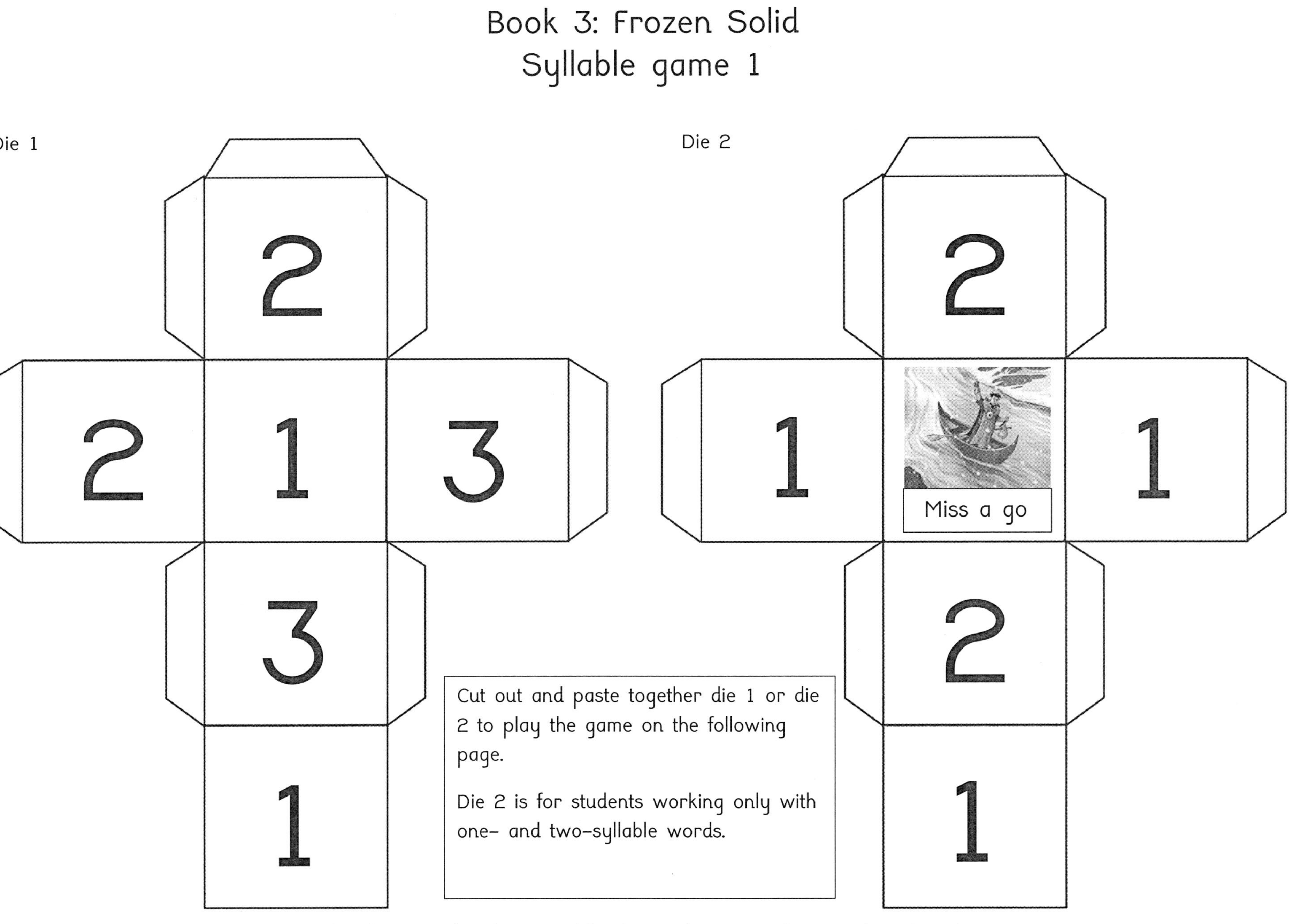

Cut out and paste together die 1 or die 2 to play the game on the following page.

Die 2 is for students working only with one- and two-syllable words.

Book 3: Frozen Solid

Syllable game 2

joke	snowman	follower
road	shadow	envelope
grow	hopeful	bungalow
toe	rotate	borrowing
so	below	composer
show	approach	telescope

A game for 2 to 4 players

Photocopy this page onto card and cut the words out. Write the number of syllables in each word on the back of each card. For ease, the words have been arranged here in columns of one-, two- and three-syllable words. Use only the first two columns of cards for students working with just one- and two-syllable words. Turn the cards word-side up and mix up on a table.

Players take it in turns to roll the die and find a word that has the corresponding number of syllables. The player turns over the card they have selected to check they are right. If they are right, they keep the card. If not, the card is turned over again and remains in play.

Book 3: Frozen Solid

Phonic patterns

Colour in the words with 'oe' spellings.

wrote	long	nod	hope
wobble	coast	foggy	loaf
bone	hop	pillow	show
nose	stop	oblong	often
soap	floppy	yellow	no

Fold this sheet along the dotted line. Read the words in the column on the left. Listen to the sounds in the words. Colour in the boxes with words that have 'oe' spellings. Repeat this with the other columns. Unfold the sheet and check that the correct words have been coloured in.

Book 3: Frozen Solid

Is it true?

Mina and Bain spot an egg floating in the stream. It is in a basket. A man is swimming in the stream, chasing the egg. He throws snowballs at the egg.

Mina and Bain follow the egg as it floats in the stream. It begins to snow. The stream opens into a frozen lake. Mina jumps onto the frozen lake. She jumps from tree trunk to tree trunk to try and reach the egg. The man in the boat jumps out onto the ice too!

Mina has a plan. She throws Bain a rope. Bain uses the rope to tie the man up! Mina and Bain grab the egg and race to a cave. They are both lovely and hot.

There are 6 things in the story above that are not true. Can you spot them?

Ask the student to read the text carefully and circle any false information that has been planted in the story.

This sheet can be cut or folded along the dotted line before presenting to the student.

- -

6 things that are not true:

The egg is not in a basket. A man is not swimming in the stream. The man does not throw snowballs at the egg. Mina does not jump from tree trunk to tree trunk. Bain does not use the rope to tie the man up. Mina and Bain are not lovely and hot.

Book 3: Frozen Solid

Retelling the story

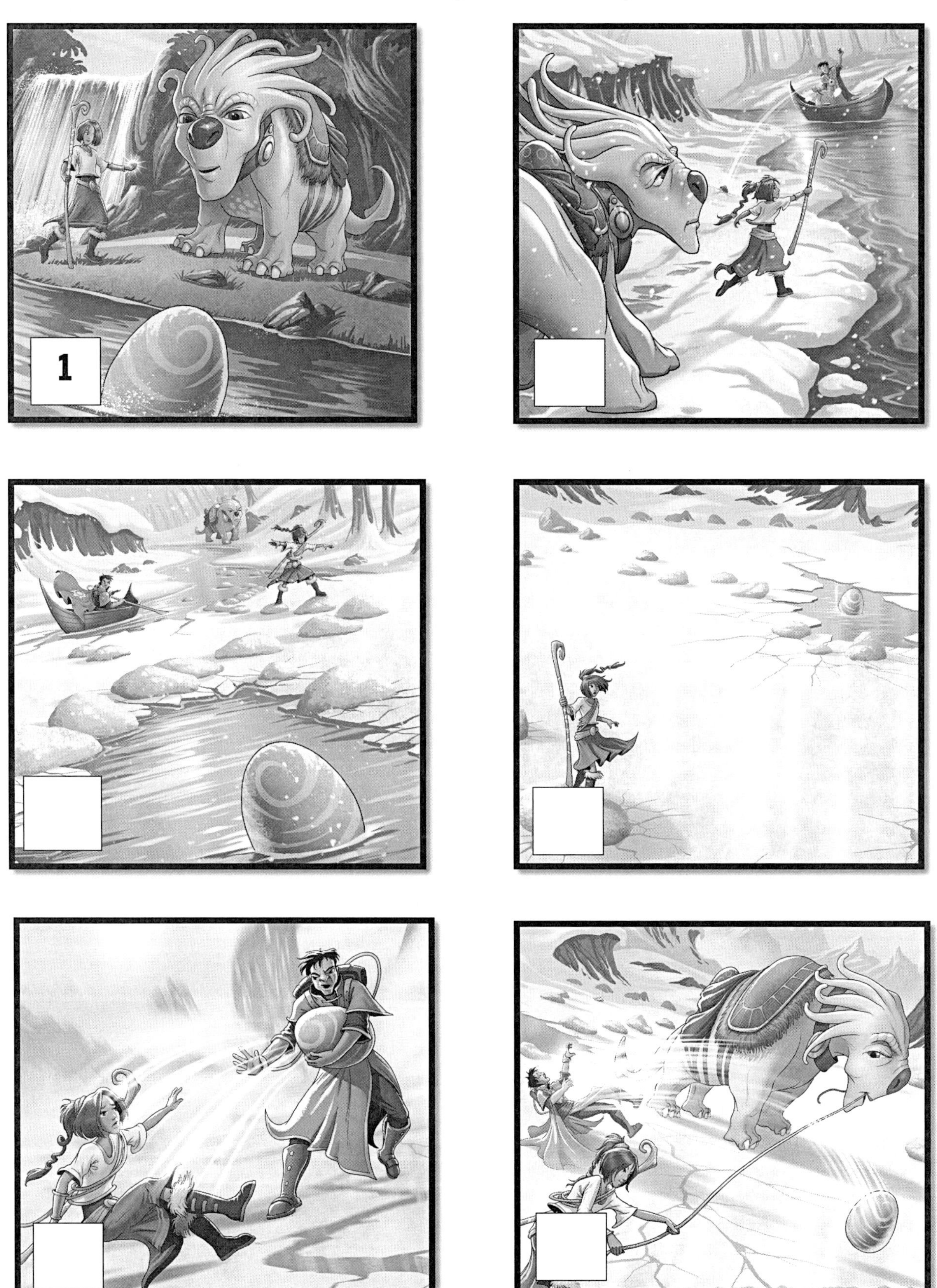

Use the story cards to sequence and tell the story.
Can be used as either an oral or a written activity. The teacher can choose whether to number any of cards 2 to 6.

Book 3: Frozen Solid

Picture the scene

Mina is in the bottom left-hand side of the picture.

She is standing on a rock.

The egg is in the top right-hand side of the picture. It is stuck in a hole in the ice.

The egg has cracks all around it.

There are six rocks between Mina and the egg.

Ask the student to read the text carefully and draw the details of the picture as described in the text. Remind the student to read all the instructions through once before starting drawing.

Book 3: Frozen Solid

Dictation

It began to __ __ ___.   A strong wind swept the egg away from the man in the __ ___ __.

"__ __!" he yelled.

He grabbed some __ __ __ __ __ __ from a sack in the __ ___ __.   He began to ___ __ ___ them at the egg!

He was trying to push it to the bank.

Mina and Bain ran along the __ __ ___ __ bank of the stream, __ __ ___ ___ __ ___ the __ ___ __.

Use the text at the bottom of the page for dictation. The section for dictation can either be cut off by the teacher or be folded along the dotted line to allow the student to self-check their spellings on completion. Dictate the passage to the student. Ask her/him to spell the missing words, writing a sound on each line. Explain that longer lines indicate spellings with more than one letter, e.g. r ow.

It began to <u>s</u> <u>n</u> <u>ow</u>.   A strong wind swept the egg away from the man in the <u>b</u> <u>oa</u> <u>t</u>.

"<u>N</u> <u>o</u>!" he yelled.

He grabbed some <u>s</u> <u>t</u> <u>o</u> <u>n</u> <u>e</u> <u>s</u> from a sack in the <u>b</u> <u>oa</u> <u>t</u>. He began to <u>th</u> <u>r</u> <u>ow</u> them at the egg! He was trying to push it to the bank.

Mina and Bain ran along the <u>s</u> <u>n</u> <u>ow</u> <u>y</u> bank of the stream, <u>f</u> <u>o</u> <u>ll</u> <u>ow</u> <u>i</u> <u>ng</u> the <u>b</u> <u>oa</u> <u>t</u>.

Book 3: Frozen Solid

Developing vocabulary: **focus**

The word 'focus' is used here in Book 3:

'focus' means: to concentrate or pay attention to something

Circle the word or phrase that could be replaced with the word 'focus' in the following text:

It was dark inside the hall and very hot. Marvin tried to concentrate on what Bella was saying. He couldn't hear much over the music.

Can you write two different sentences of your own using the word 'focus'?

1.

____

____

2.

____

____

Book 3: Frozen Solid

Reading fluency

Mina rode on Bain's back as they followed the stream inland. She began to feel cold.

"We need a safe place to stop and sleep," Mina told Bain. "Let's just get the next egg. Then we can stop and rest."

The gem in Mina's hand began to glow gold.

"It's showing us the way!" yelled Mina.

Suddenly, Bain stopped. What had he seen?

Mina gasped. The next egg was floating along next to them in the stream!

A man in a boat rowed quickly past them.

He was very close to the golden egg.

"He's closing in on it!" yelled Mina. "We have to stop him!"

The man had an odd shape printed on the back of his coat. What did it mean?

Ask the student to read through the passage to familiarise themselves with the text.
Read it through for them again to model reading with expression and attention to punctuation.
Ask the student to read the passage again, thinking about adding expression to their reading and following punctuation in the passage. Students who struggle with punctuation may benefit from highlighting the punctuation in the text before reading.
Teachers can fold the page to cover the bottom paragraph of text to offer a shorter passage if needed.

Book 3: Frozen Solid

Make a page for a comic – reading comprehension

1

Mina and Bain follow a stream inland. They spot a gold egg bobbing in the stream.

2

A man in a boat is following the egg! He throws stones at the egg, and then at Mina!

3

The egg floats into a frozen lake and gets stuck in the ice. Mina and the man both jump onto the ice to try and reach the egg.

4

Mina and Bain trip up the man with a rope and escape with the egg!

Ask the student to read the text and draw a picture to match the text in each box.

Book 3: Frozen Solid

Dice game: words with 'oe' spellings

⚀	⚁	⚂	⚃	⚄	⚅
so	code	goat	roast	zone	toad
row	slope	below	joking	follow	boast
toes	moan	stone	pillow	rope	slow
cope	show	blow	bone	throne	no
most	crow	wrote	foam	go	choke

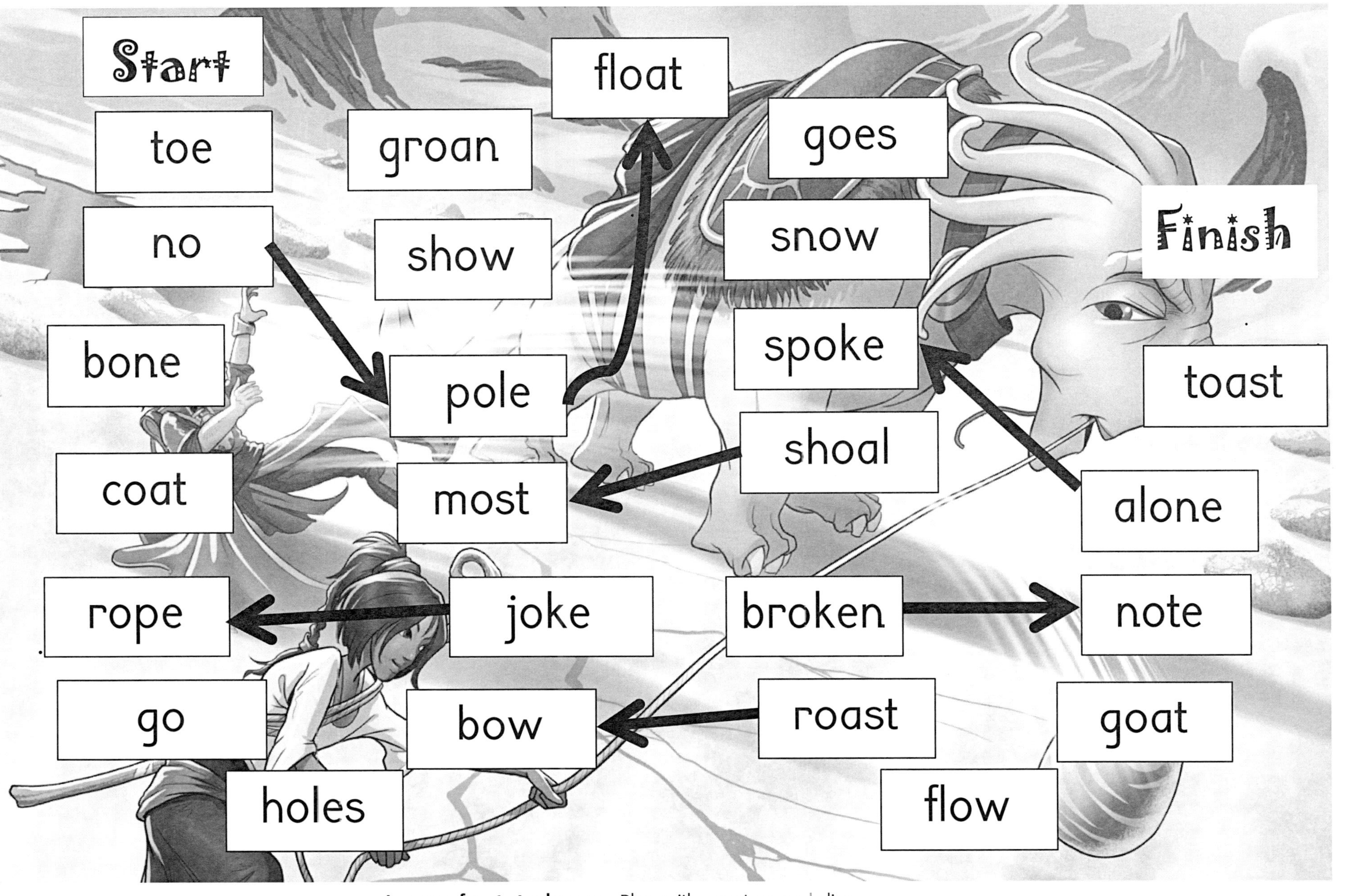

A game for 1–4 players: Play with counters and dice.
Players should read aloud the words that they land on at the end of each turn and follow the direction arrows if they land on them.

This sheet may be photocopied by the purchaser. © Phonic Books Ltd 2021

Book 3: Frozen Solid

Spelling assessment: words with 'oe' spellings

1.

oa	ow	o–e	o	oe
road	low	rope	no	toe
coast	show	spoke	go	hoe
broach	flown	choke	post	woe

2.

oa	ow	o–e	o	oe
boastful	window	lonely	rodent	tiptoe
floated	shadow	hopeful	hotel	woeful
groaning	slowly			

These lists can be used as a spelling assessment at the end of each book. The teacher can add words from list 2 for students who are ready for that stage. When dictating a word, first say the word on its own. Next, say a sentence with the word in it (to put the word in the context of a sentence) and then repeat the word. This ensures that the student has understood the word correctly, e.g. "Hope. I hope the train isn't late. Hope."

Book 4: The Sky Worm
Contents

Book 4: The Sky Worm

Blending and segmenting: 'er'

sir	s	ir	
her			
word			
earn			
twirl			
church			
learn			
worth			
term			
world			
skirt			
burst			

Blend the sounds into a word. Segment the word into sounds by writing one sound in each square.

Book 4: The Sky Worm

Reading and sorting words with 'er' spellings

er	**ur**	**ir**	**or**	**ear**

her	early	dirty	stir
world	bird	verse	disturb
earn	serve	worse	under
purse	turn	work	hurtle
jerk	worth	learn	sister
first	heard	curse	stir
burp	curl	word	expert
worm	kerb	birth	herd

Photocopy this page onto card and cut out the words. Read and sort the cards out according to the 'er' headings at the top of the page.

Book 4: The Sky Worm

Reading and spelling words with 'er' spellings

<table>
<tr><td>er</td><td>ur</td><td>ir</td></tr>
</table>

<table>
<tr><td>or</td><td>ear</td></tr>
</table>

worm	first	burp	butter	world	earn	purse	bird
serve	helper	turn	birth	heard	dirty	work	
sister	verb	earth	churn	girl	fur		

List the words according to the 'er' spellings.

Book 4: The Sky Worm

Timed reading of words with 'er' spellings

firm   burn   verse   worse   term   worm   skirt

germ   heard   father   church   over   enter

search   early   dirt   sister   shirt   fern

1st try   **Time:**

- -

firm   burn   verse   worse   term   worm   skirt

germ   heard   father   church   over   enter

search   early   dirt   sister   shirt   fern

2nd try   **Time:**

- -

firm   burn   verse   worse   term   worm   skirt

germ   heard   father   church   over   enter

search   early   dirt   sister   shirt   fern

3rd try   **Time:**

This timed reading activity is for the student to improve her/his reading speed and fluency. Ask the student to read the words as fast as she/he can. Record the time in the box. Repeat the activity This sheet can be cut or folded along the dotted lines to allow for different presentations.

Book 4: The Sky Worm

Chunking two-syllable words with 'er' spellings

disturb	dis	turb	disturb
worthless			
permit			
further			
birthday			
worker			
early			
worship			
expert			
thirsty			
murder			
learning			
thirteen			
burning			

Split the word into two syllables. Write each syllable in a box.
Write the whole word while saying the syllables. This worksheet allows the student to use the
approach she/he has been taught for splitting words.

Book 4: The Sky Worm
Syllable game 1

Die 1

Die 2

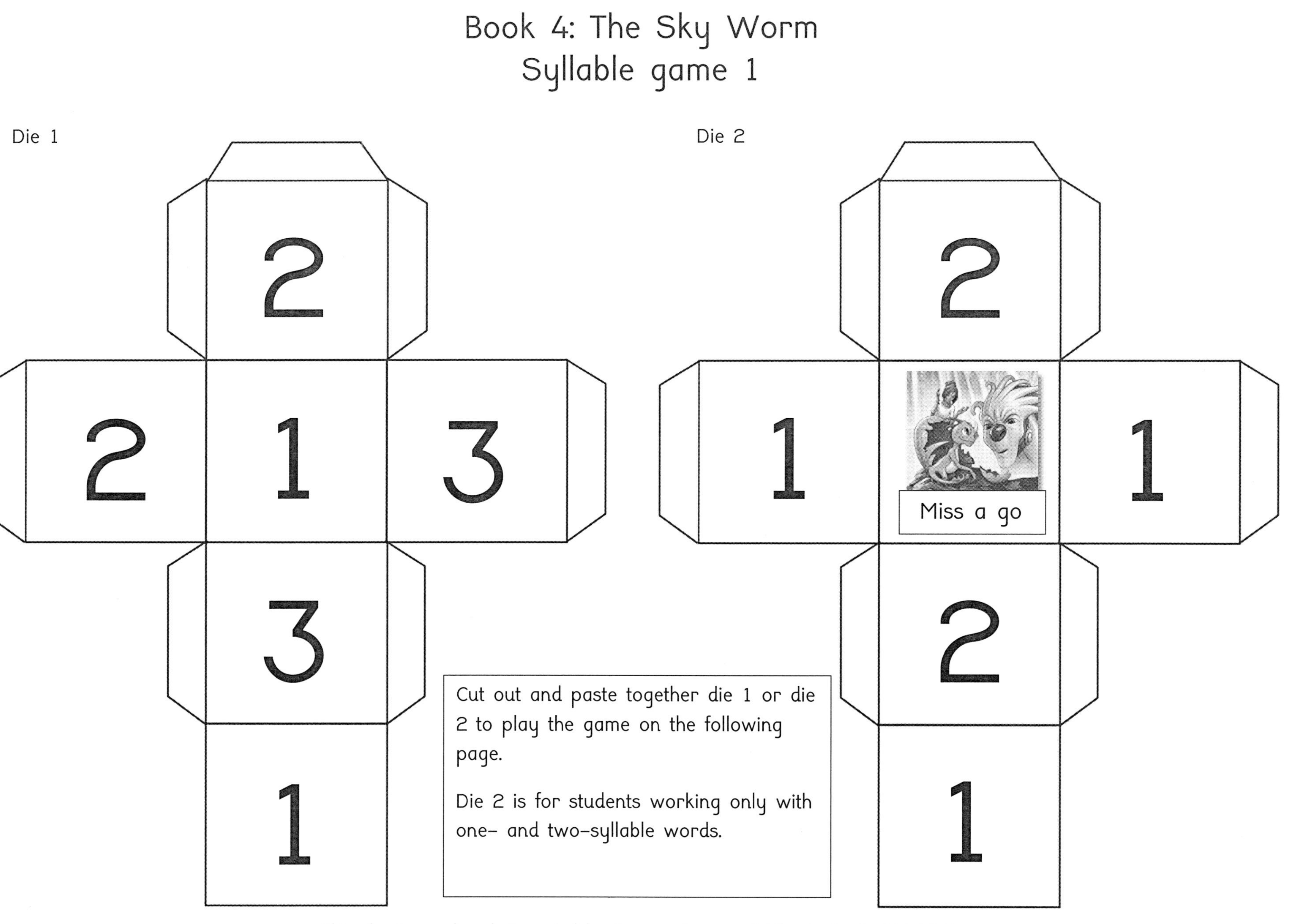

Cut out and paste together die 1 or die 2 to play the game on the following page.

Die 2 is for students working only with one- and two-syllable words.

This sheet may be photocopied by the purchaser. © Phonic Books Ltd 2021

Book 4: The Sky Worm

Syllable game 2

burn	disturb	follower
third	further	observer
learn	learning	returning
word	wordless	surgery
her	sister	eternal
fir	birdbath	interest

A game for 2 to 4 players

Photocopy this page onto card and cut the words out. Write the number of syllables in each word on the back of each card. For ease, the words have been arranged here in columns of one-, two- and three-syllable words. Use only the first two columns of cards for students working with just one- and two-syllable words. Turn the cards word-side up and mix up on a table.

Players take it in turns to roll the die and find a word that has the corresponding number of syllables. The player turns over the card they have selected to check they are right. If they are right, they keep the card. If not, the card is turned over again and remains in play.

Book 4: The Sky Worm

Phonic patterns

Colour in the words with 'er' spellings.

butter	bundle	yellow	search
blend	serve	greet	bendy
head	stumble	sister	stir
first	turn	rest	worship
world	fresh	worm	early

Fold this sheet along the dotted line. Read the words in the column on the left. Listen to the sounds in the words. Colour in the boxes with words that have 'er' spellings. Repeat this with the other columns. Unfold the sheet and check that the correct words have been coloured in.

This sheet may be photocopied by the purchaser. © Phonic Books Ltd 2021

Book 4: The Sky Worm

Is it true?

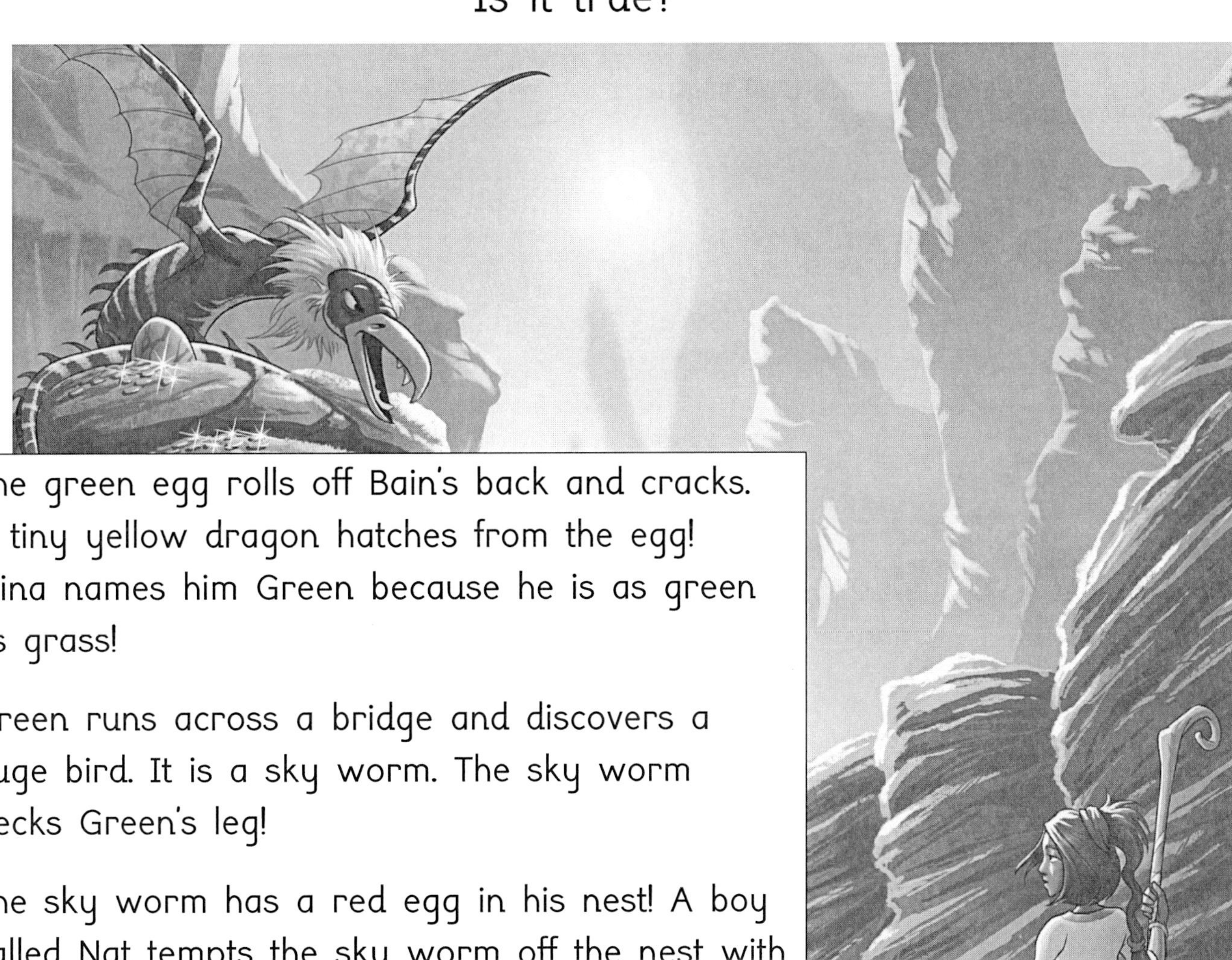

The green egg rolls off Bain's back and cracks. A tiny yellow dragon hatches from the egg! Mina names him Green because he is as green as grass!

Green runs across a bridge and discovers a huge bird. It is a sky worm. The sky worm pecks Green's leg!

The sky worm has a red egg in his nest! A boy called Nat tempts the sky worm off the nest with a trail of cake crumbs.

Green runs in circles and makes the sky worm dizzy. The sky worm bangs his head and faints.

Nat wishes them good luck and says goodbye.

There are 8 things in the story above that are not true. Can you spot them?

Ask the student to read the text carefully and circle any false information that has been planted in the story.

This sheet can be cut or folded along the dotted line before presenting to the student.

- -

8 things that are not true:

A yellow dragon does not hatch from the egg. Mina does not name the dragon Green because he is as green as grass. Green does not run across a bridge. The sky worm does not peck Green's leg. There is not a red egg in the nest. Nat does not tempt the sky worm off the nest with a trail of cake crumbs. The sky worm does not bang his head and faint. Nat does not say goodbye.

Book 4: The Sky Worm

Retelling the story

Use the story cards to sequence and tell the story.
Can be used as either an oral or a written activity. The teacher can choose whether to number any of cards 2 to 6.

Book 4: The Sky Worm

Picture the scene

A broken egg shell is in the front left-hand side of the picture.

A baby green dragon is next to the egg shell.

Mina is behind the dragon. She has her arms up in the air and is smiling.

Bain's face is in one corner of the picture.

Ask the student to read the text carefully and draw the details of the picture as described in the text. Remind the student to read all the instructions through once before starting drawing.

Book 4: The Sky Worm

Dictation

Green   __ ____ __ ____   the   __ ____ __ ____   egg out

of the nest. He pushed the egg down to the boy!

The sky   __ ____ __   __ ____ __   him and it   __ ___ __ ____

round!

"He's going to catch him!" screamed Mina.

But Green was   __ __ __ __ ____.   He ran in

__ ____ __ __ __   round the   __ ____ __.   The   __ ____ __

twisted and   __ ____ __ ____.

- -

Use the text at the bottom of the page for dictation. The section for dictation can either be cut off by the teacher or be folded along the dotted line to allow the student to self-check their spellings on completion. Dictate the passage to the student. Ask her/him to spell the missing words, writing a sound on each line. Explain that longer lines indicate spellings with more than one letter, e.g. <u>h</u> <u>er</u>

Green   <u>w</u> <u>or</u> <u>k</u> <u>ed</u>   the   <u>p</u> <u>ur</u> <u>p</u> <u>le</u>   egg out of the nest. He pushed the egg down to the boy!

The sky   <u>w</u> <u>or</u> <u>m</u>   <u>h</u> <u>ear</u> <u>d</u>   him and it   <u>t</u> <u>ur</u> <u>n</u> <u>ed</u>   round.

"He's going to catch him!" screamed Mina.

But Green was   <u>c</u> <u>l</u> <u>e</u> <u>v</u> <u>er</u>.   He ran in   <u>c</u> <u>ir</u> <u>c</u> <u>le</u> <u>s</u>   round the   <u>b</u> <u>ir</u> <u>d</u>.   The   <u>b</u> <u>ir</u> <u>d</u>

twisted and   <u>t</u> <u>ur</u> <u>n</u> <u>ed</u>.

Book 4: The Sky Worm

Developing vocabulary: **lurched**

The word 'lurched" is used here in Book 4:

'lurched' means: swayed or staggered

Circle the word or phrase that could be replaced with the word 'lurched' in the following text:

> The little cat's ears pricked up. He had heard the dog.
> The dog jumped at the cat. The cat hissed. It was a loud,
> sharp sound. The dog staggered backwards, shocked.

Can you write two different sentences of your own using the word 'lurched'?

1.

____

____

2.

____

____

Reading fluency

Mina and Bain gazed in wonder. First they saw a little green leg… then a tiny folded wing. Slowly a little baby dragon worked its way out of the broken egg shell!

"You're as green as a plate of peas!" grinned Mina. "Let's name you Green!"

Green stretched and giggled happily. He sniffed at the dirt and sneezed! Then he set off across the rocky path.

"I think he's keen to see the world!" said Mina.

Green was a quick learner and a very fast runner. He soon reached the edge of a steep cliff. Mina began to panic.

"Quick, Bain, we must catch up with him in case he falls over the top!"

Suddenly Green lurched back with a whimper. A massive bird whirled up in front of them, screeching in anger.

Ask the student to read through the passage to familiarise themselves with the text.
Read it through for them again to model reading with expression and attention to punctuation.
Ask the student to read the passage again, thinking about adding expression to their reading and following punctuation in the passage. Students who struggle with punctuation may benefit from highlighting the punctuation in the text before reading.
Teachers can fold the page to cover the bottom paragraph of text to offer a shorter passage if needed.

Book 4: The Sky Worm

Make a page for a comic – reading comprehension

1

A little baby dragon as green as peas hatches out of the green egg! He runs off to explore.

2

Green discovers a huge bird. It is a sky worm! The sky worm has a purple egg in his nest.

3

A boy called Nat helps Green to rescue the purple egg from the sky worm. The sky worm spins in giant circles in the air trying to catch Green.

4

The purple egg is safe, thanks to Nat and Green. Nat asks if he can join Mina and Bain on their quest to save the rest of the dragon eggs.

Ask the student to read the text and draw a picture to match the text in each box.

Book 4: The Sky Worm

Dice game: words with 'er' spellings

1	2	3	4	5	6
term	kerb	burp	jerk	turf	spider
worm	sister	world	shirt	word	purple
skirt	fur	learn	yearn	first	hurt
firm	early	bird	work	earn	girl
worth	dirty	fern	turn	worst	burst

This game is for two players. Each player needs a batch of counters of one colour. The players take turns to throw the die. They read a word in the column that corresponds to the number on the die and place their counter on that word. The first to have three of her/his counters in a row in any direction is the winner. This sheet may be photocopied by the purchaser. © Phonic Books Ltd 2021

Book 4: The Sky Worm   Stepping stones reading game: 'er' words

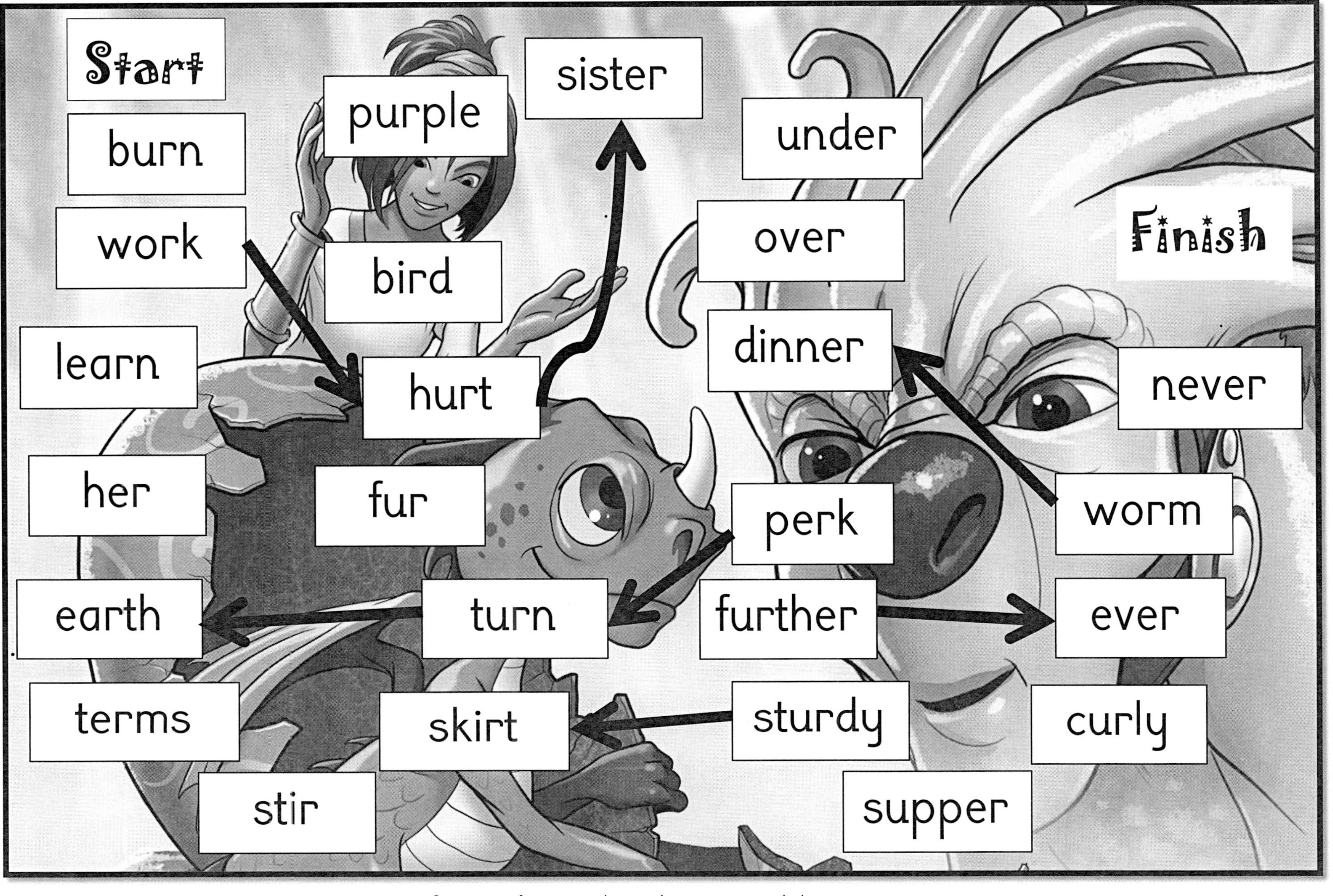

A game for 1–4 players: Play with counters and dice. Players should read aloud the words that they land on at the end of each turn and follow the direction arrows if they land on them.

This sheet may be photocopied by the purchaser. © Phonic Books Ltd 2021

Book 4: The Sky Worm

Spelling assessment: words with 'er' spellings

1.

er	ir	ur	ear	or
her	sir	turn	earn	word
term	bird	churn	pearl	worth
stern	stir	burns	heard	worms

2.

er	ir	ur	ear	or
over	shirt	church	search	world
supper	twirl	disturb	learned	worst
fingers	birthday	curling	earnest	worthless

These lists can be used as a spelling assessment at the end of each book. The teacher can add words from list 2 for students who are ready for that stage. When dictating a word, first say the word on its own. Next, say a sentence with the word in it (to put the word in the context of a sentence) and then repeat the word. This ensures that the student has understood the word correctly, e.g. "Shirt. The boy had a red shirt on. Shirt."

Book 5: Lost and Found
Contents

Book 5: Lost and Found
Contents

Book 5: Lost and Found

Blending and segmenting: 'ow' and 'oi'

how	h	ow			
out					
loud					
town					
mouth					
howling					
oil					
toy					
enjoy					
coin					
toilet					
employ					

Blend the sounds into a word. Segment the word into sounds by writing one sound in each square.

Book 5: Lost and Found

Reading and sorting words with 'ow' and 'oi' spellings

| **ow** | **ou** |

out	now	owl	foul
howl	round	aloud	tower
allow	spout	shower	sound
pouch	power	shout	frown

| **oi** | **oy** |

boy	point	destroy	foil
soil	toys	loyal	voice
decoy	coin	annoy	spoilt

Photocopy this page onto card and cut out the words. Read and sort the cards out according to the 'ow' and 'oi' headings.

Book 5: Lost and Found

Reading and spelling words with 'ow' and 'oi' spellings

ow	ou
______	______
______	______
______	______
______	______

howl   outing   around   clown   cloud   towel

fountain   flower

oy	oi
______	______
______	______
______	______
______	______

toy   spoil   enjoy   point   ploy   foil

avoid   boy

List the words according to the 'ow' and 'oi' spellings.

Book 5: Lost and Found

Timed reading of words with 'ow' spellings

cow	loud	round	town	pout	house	mound
allow	proud	howl	how	crowd	noun	
sound	vowel	spout	frown	brow	mouse	

1st try   **Time:**

- -

cow	loud	round	town	pout	house	mound
allow	proud	howl	how	crowd	noun	
sound	vowel	spout	frown	brow	mouse	

2nd try   **Time:**

- -

cow	loud	round	town	pout	house	mound
allow	proud	howl	how	crowd	noun	
sound	vowel	spout	frown	brow	mouse	

3rd try   **Time:**

This timed reading activity is for the student to improve her/his reading speed and fluency. Ask the student to read the words as fast as she/he can. Record the time in the box. Repeat the activity. This sheet can be cut or folded along the dotted lines to allow for different presentations.

Book 5: Lost and Found

Timed reading of words with 'oi' spellings

boy   noise   toy   spoil   soya   boil   voice

joy   coin   oyster   annoy   coil   point

oil   joint   poise   ointment   employ   boiling

1st try   **Time:**

boy   noise   toy   spoil   soya   boil   voice

joy   coin   oyster   annoy   coil   point

oil   joint   poise   ointment   employ   boiling

2nd try   **Time:**

boy   noise   toy   spoil   soya   boil   voice

joy   coin   oyster   annoy   coil   point

oil   joint   poise   ointment   employ   boiling

3rd try   **Time:**

This timed reading activity is for the student to improve her/his reading speed and fluency. Ask the student to read the words as fast as she/he can. Record the time in the box. Repeat the activity. This sheet can be cut or folded along the dotted lines to allow for different presentations.

Book 5: Lost and Found

Chunking two-syllable words with 'ow' spellings

power	pow	er	power
loudest			
pouting			
drowsy			
voucher			
outing			
grounded			
towel			
flower			
mouthful			
crowded			
shower			
counter			
fountain			

Split the word into two syllables. Write each syllable in a box.
Write the whole word while saying the syllables. This worksheet allows the student to use the approach she/he has been taught for splitting 'words.

Book 5: Lost and Found

Chunking two-syllable words with 'oi' spellings

enjoy	*en*	*joy*	*enjoy*
oily			
convoy			
poison			
toilet			
destroy			
avoid			
decoy			
noisy			
annoy			
boiling			
royal			
ointment			
enjoy			

Split the word into two syllables. Write each syllable in a box.
Write the whole word while saying the syllables. This worksheet allows the student to use the
approach she/he has been taught for splitting words.

Book 5: Lost and Found
Syllable game 1

Die 1

2
2 1 3
3
1

Die 2

2
1 Miss a go
1
2
1

Cut out and paste together die 1 or die 2 to play the game on the following page.

Die 2 is for students working only with one- and two-syllable words.

Book 5: Lost and Found

Syllable game 2

house	employ	allowance
clown	toilet	cowardly
foil	shower	towering
toy	voucher	accountant
round	flower	joyfully
spoil	ointment	boyishly

A game for 2 to 4 players

Photocopy this page onto card and cut the words out. Write the number of syllables in each word on the back of each card. For ease, the words have been arranged here in columns of one-, two- and three-syllable words. Use only the first two columns of cards for students working with just one- and two-syllable words. Turn the cards word-side up and mix up on a table.

Players take it in turns to roll the die and find a word that has the corresponding number of syllables. The player turns over the card they have selected to check they are right. If they are right, they keep the card. If not, the card is turned over again and remains in play.

Book 5: Lost and Found

Phonic patterns

Colour in <u>only</u> the words with the spelling **ow** that is pronounced 'ow' as in 'clown'.

throw	frown	yellow	town
brown	growl	below	towel
grow	follow	tower	flower
crown	shower	cow	blow
allow	down	slow	snow

Fold this sheet along the dotted line. Read the words in the column on the left. Listen to the sounds in the words. Colour in the boxes with words that have 'ow' spellings. Repeat this with the other columns. Unfold the sheet and check that the correct words have been coloured in.
This sheet may be photocopied by the purchaser. © Phonic Books Ltd 2021

Book 5: Lost and Found

Reading and sorting words with 'ow' spellings

ow as in sn**ow**		**ow** as in c**ow**	
now	blow	low	tow
howl	growl	mow	grow
flow	know	crown	crow
allow	glow	brow	town
slow	show	brown	fowl
jowl	power	bowl	howl
vow	throw	trowel	towel
down	shower	yellow	flower

Photocopy this page onto card and cut out the words. Read and sort the cards out
according to the 'ow' headings at the top of the page.

This sheet may be photocopied by the purchaser. © Phonic Books Ltd 2021

Book 5: Lost and Found

Is it true?

Nat takes Mina to a place by the river. He shows her a wrecked cabin he has found. They hear some men singing loudly. Nat explains that they are bounty hunters looking for the dragon eggs!

The men have a big grey dog with them. He chases after Green. Nat and Green hide behind a tree. One of the hunters chases Mina. She manages to escape by dropping some gems on the floor for him to pick up.

Bain chases the big dog away. Nat and Mina climb up a cliff. They push a big barrel over the top of the cliff. The bounty hunters are caught up in a fountain of nails that bursts out of the barrel!

There are 7 things in the story above that are not true. Can you spot them?

Ask the student to read the text carefully and circle any false information that has been planted in the story.

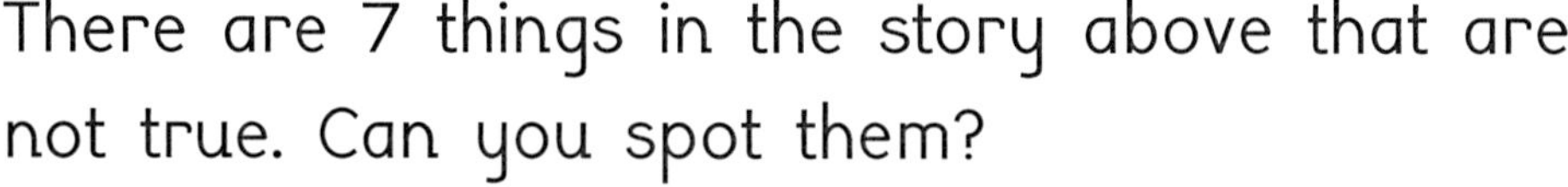

This sheet can be cut or folded along the dotted line before presenting to the student.

7 things that are not true:

Nat does not take Mina to a place by the river. Nat does not show Mina a wrecked cabin. They do not hear some men singing loudly. The men do not have a big grey dog. Nat and Green do not hide behind a tree. Mina does not escape by dropping some gems on the floor. The bounty hunters are not caught up in a fountain of nails.

Book 5: Lost and Found

Retelling the story

Use the story cards to sequence and tell the story.
Can be used as either an oral or a written activity. The teacher can choose whether to number any of cards 2 to 6.

Book 5: Lost and Found

Picture the scene

There is a barrel in the middle of the picture.

Nat and Green are hiding behind the barrel, at the front of the picture.

A big dog is sniffing the ground at the other end of the barrel.

The edge of the sea and three trees are at the back of the picture.

Ask the student to read the text carefully and draw the details of the picture as described in the text. Remind the student to read all the instructions through once before starting drawing.

Book 5: Lost and Found

Dictation

Green ran across the beach making a __ ____ __

__ ____ __ __ ____ __ ____ ___! The __ __ ____ __ dog

was __ ____ ____ ____. He chased after the baby dragon,

__ ____ __ __ ____. Nat ran too. He got to Green first and

snatched him up from the __ __ ____ __ __.

The hunters had spotted Mina. One of them stuffed the

__ __ ____ __ egg into a __ ____ ____. The other one ran

after Mina. __ ____ was she going to slow him __ ____ __?

Use the text at the bottom of the page for dictation. The section for dictation can either be cut off by the teacher or be folded along the dotted line to allow the student to self-check their spellings on completion. Dictate the passage to the student. Ask her/him to spell the missing words, writing a sound on each line. Explain that longer lines indicate spellings with more than one letter, e.g. c ow.

Green ran across the beach making a **l ou d**   **h ow l i ng**   **n oi se** ! The   **b r ow n** dog was **a nn oy ed**.   He chased after the baby dragon,   **h ow l i ng**.   Nat ran too. He got to Green first and snatched him up from the   **g r ou n d**.

The hunters had spotted Mina. One of them stuffed the   **b r ow n**   egg into a   **p ou ch**. The other one ran after Mina. **H ow** was she going to slow him   **d ow n** ?

Book 5: Lost and Found

Developing vocabulary: **scout**

The word 'scout' is used here in Book 5:

'scout' means: to search or hunt

Circle the word or phrase that could be replaced with the word 'scout' in the following text:

Tess was hungry. It had been a very long time since lunch. "Time to hunt round the kitchen cupboards and see if I can find some cake!" she told the cat with a grin.

Can you write two different sentences of your own using the word 'scout'?

1.

____

____

2.

____

____

Book 5: Lost and Found

Reading fluency

"I think I have a plan," Mina told Nat. "Can you help me push that barrel off the cliff, Nat?"

The barrel of fish bounced down the cliff. It landed with a smack, next to the two unlucky hunters. A fountain of fish and water spouted out of it and drenched them. Yuck! It smelled foul.

The hunters staggered about. They dropped the egg. It spun round and round, just out of reach. Their plan had been spoiled. They were trapped in the fishy mess!

Mina and Nat grabbed the egg and quickly escaped.

"That fishy plan was disgusting, but it really worked!" said Nat with a grin as they set up camp. It had been a long day. As they settled down to sleep, they missed a tiny cracking sound. They didn't know it yet, but the purple and golden eggs had begun to hatch!

Ask the student to read through the passage to familiarise themselves with the text.
Read it through for them again to model reading with expression and attention to punctuation.
Ask the student to read the passage again, thinking about adding expression to their reading and following punctuation in the passage. Students who struggle with punctuation may benefit from highlighting the punctuation in the text before reading.
Teachers can fold the page to cover the bottom paragraph of text to offer a shorter passage if needed.

Book 5: Lost and Found

Make a page for a comic – reading comprehension

1

Nat takes Mina and Green to a beach. Mina finds a pouch of coins in an old shipwreck.

2

Two men have found a brown egg on the beach. Nat explains they are bounty hunters.

3

A huge brown dog chases Green. Nat hides behind a barrel with Green. Mina distracts the bounty hunters with the coins she found on the shipwreck.

4

Nat and Mina push a barrel of oily fish over a cliff and it explodes! The bounty hunters are covered in fishy oil. Mina and Nat rescue the brown egg.

Ask the student to read the text and draw a picture to match the text in each box.

Book 5: Lost and Found

Dice game: words with 'ow' and 'oi' spellings

1	2	3	4	5	6
loud	toil	fowl	round	toy	noise
out	town	spout	house	spoil	boy
boil	mount	allow	voice	proud	howl
coin	poise	annoy	crowd	point	sound
royal	owl	towel	noun	soil	loyal

This game is for two players. Each player needs a batch of counters of one colour. The players take turns to throw the die. They read a word in the column that corresponds to the number on the die and place their counter on that word. The first to have three of her/his counters in a row in any direction is the winner.

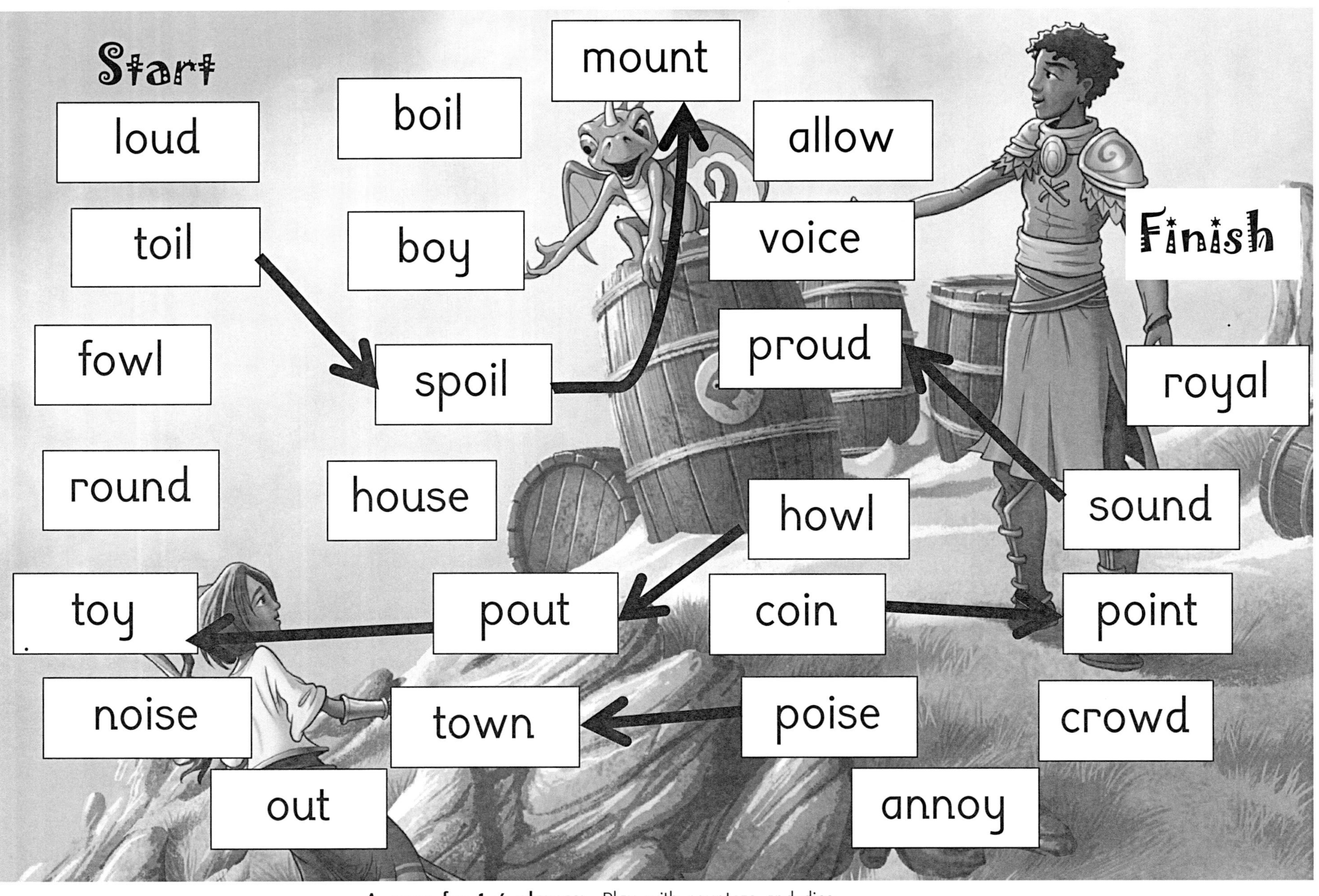

A game for 1–4 players: Play with counters and dice.
Players should read aloud the words that they land on at the end of each turn and follow the direction arrows if they land on them.

Book 5: Lost and Found

Spelling assessment: words with 'ow' and 'oi' spellings

1.

ow	ou	oy	oi
cow	out	boy	coin
down	pout	toy	spoil
clown	sound	royal	point

2.

ow	ou	oy	oi
power	loudest	oyster	avoid
towel	voucher	annoy	toilet
howling	mouthful	employ	ointment

These lists can be used as a spelling assessment at the end of each book. The teacher can add words from list 2 for students who are ready for that stage. When dictating a word, first say the word on its own. Next, say a sentence with the word in it (to put the word in the context of a sentence) and then repeat the word. This ensures that the student has understood the word correctly, e.g. "Toy. The boy gave his sister a toy. Toy."

Book 6: Confusing Routes
Contents

Book 6: Confusing Routes

Blending and segmenting: 'oo'

you

too

rude

chew

truth

clue

boot

soup

threw

rule

super

cruel

Blend the sounds into a word. Segment the word into sounds by writing one sound in each square. Split vowel spellings (u–e) are represented by half squares linked together.

Book 6: Confusing Routes

Reading and sorting words with 'oo' spellings

oo	ou	ue	u-e	ew	u

drew	proof	loose	crew
pool	rude	blue	group
grew	July	shoot	youth
flew	rule	true	brutal
glue	scoop	crude	chew
route	judo	smooth	sue
brute	jewel	include	scuba
plume	shampoo	coupon	flume

Photocopy this page onto card and cut out the words. Read and sort the cards out according to the 'oo' headings at the top of the page.

Book 6: Confusing Routes

Reading and spelling words with 'oo' spellings

<table>
<tr><td>oo</td><td>ou</td><td>ue</td></tr>
<tr><td>u–e</td><td>ew</td><td>u</td></tr>
</table>

pool   group   rude   blue   grew   brutal   shoot
youth   true   rule   flew   judo   smooth   coupon
brute   chew   July   glue   shampoo   route
gruesome   soup   scoop   clue

List the words according to the 'oo' spellings.

Timed reading of words with 'oo' spellings

you   true   rule   flew   judo   smooth   coupon

brute   chew   July   glue   shampoo   route   soup

scoop   clue   too   truth   threw

1st try   **Time:**

---

you   true   rule   flew   judo   smooth   coupon

brute   chew   July   glue   shampoo   route   soup

scoop   clue   too   truth   threw

2nd try   **Time:**

---

you   true   rule   flew   judo   smooth   coupon

brute   chew   July   glue   shampoo   route   soup

scoop   clue   too   truth   threw

3rd try   **Time:**

This timed reading activity is for the student to improve her/his reading speed and fluency. Ask the student to read the words as fast as she/he can. Record the time in the box. Repeat the activity. This sheet can be cut or folded along the dotted lines to allow for different presentations.

Chunking two-syllable words with 'oo' spellings

youthful	youth	ful	youthful
salute			
tattoo			
intrude			
gruesome			
brutal			
Andrew			
coupon			
snooker			
include			
clueless			
truthful			
chewing			
bamboo			

Split the word into two syllables. Write each syllable in a box.
Write the whole word while saying the syllables. This worksheet allows the student to use the approach she/he has been taught for splitting words.

Book 6: Confusing Routes
Syllable game 1

Die 1

Die 2

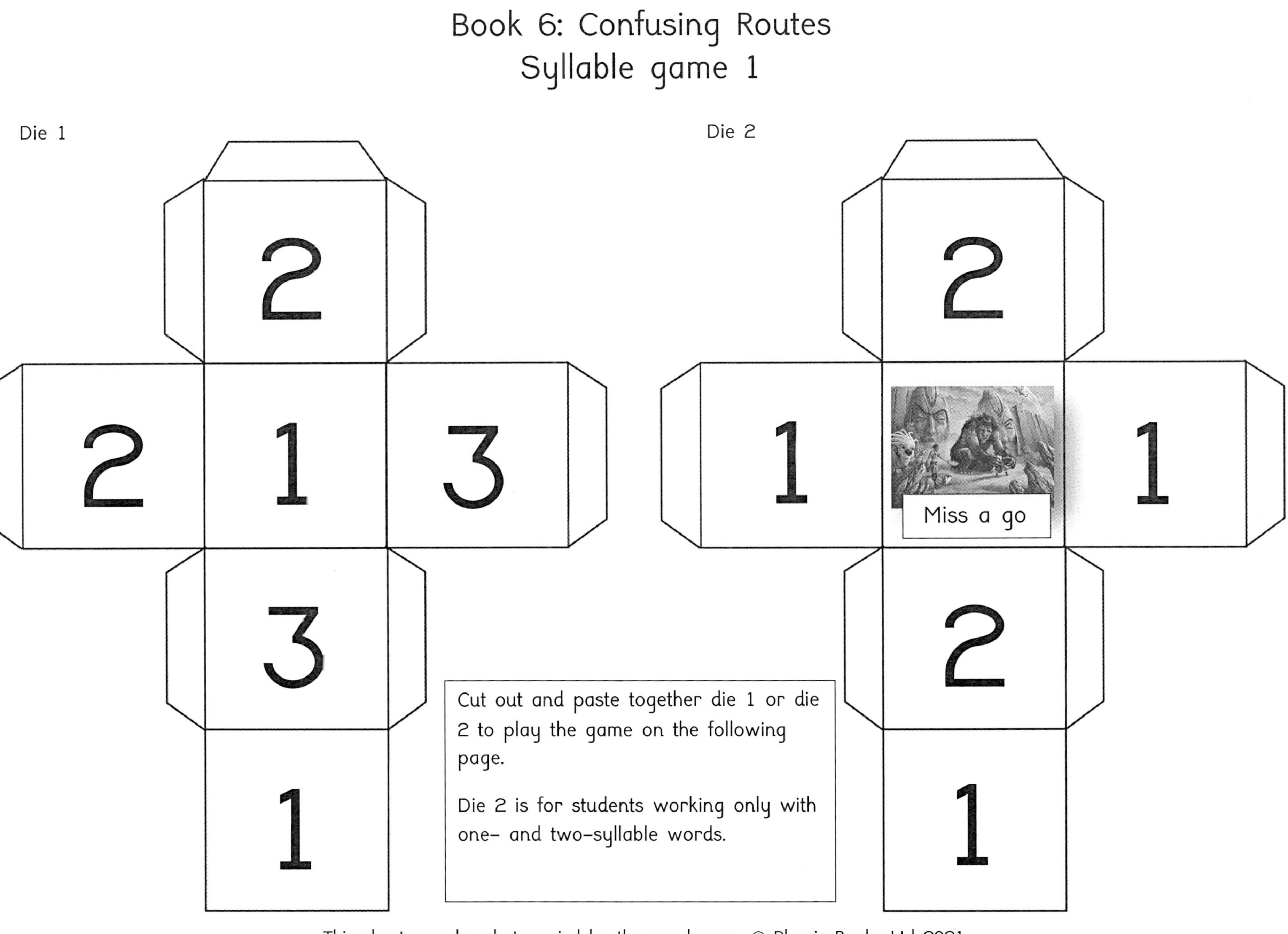

Cut out and paste together die 1 or die 2 to play the game on the following page.

Die 2 is for students working only with one- and two-syllable words.

Book 6: Confusing Routes

Syllable game 2

pool	bamboo	cartoonist
rude	youthful	cocooning
group	chewing	foolishly
true	brutal	rebooting
too	intrude	truthfully
chew	coupon	gloomily

A game for 2 to 4 players

Photocopy this page onto card and cut the words out. Write the number of syllables in each word on the back of each card. For ease, the words have been arranged here in columns of one-, two- and three-syllable words. Use only the first two columns of cards for students working with just one- and two-syllable words. Turn the cards word-side up and mix up on a table.

Players take it in turns to roll the die and find a word that has the corresponding number of syllables. The player turns over the card they have selected to check they are right. If they are right, they keep the card. If not, the card is turned over again and remains in play.

Book 6: Confusing Routes
Phonic patterns

Colour in the words with 'oo' spellings.

spook	truth	yellow	route
youth	clues	coupon	towel
angry	include	flew	tattoo
brewing	pool	brutal	flute
under	down	gruesome	snow

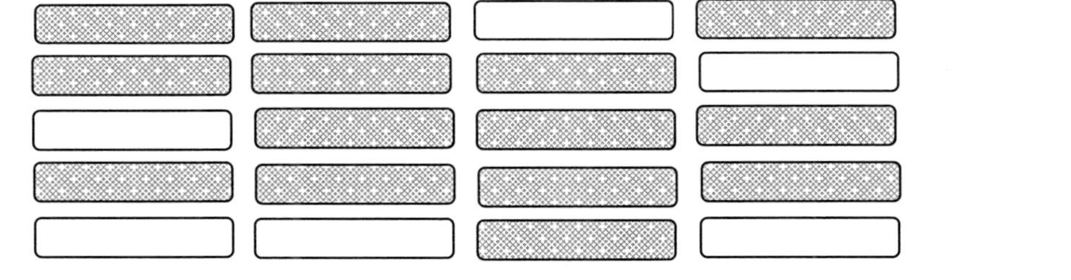

Fold this sheet along the dotted line. Read the words in the column on the left. Listen to the sounds in the words. Colour in the boxes with words that have 'oo' spellings. Repeat this with the other columns. Unfold the sheet and check that the correct words have been coloured in.

Book 6: Confusing Routes

Is it true?

The purple and gold eggs have hatched overnight! The new baby dragons are swimming in a stream. The group sets off to find the next eggs. They see a hunter running across a bridge. They follow him.

The group are seen lost in a stone maze. Gold flies high up above the stone walls of the maze and is able to see the route. They follow Gold to a room in the middle of the maze. The hunter knocks Gold out of the sky with a ball!

A huge orange beast is there! He is holding the hunter. The beast feels sorry for Gold. He whistles him a tune.

The beast leads the group safely out of the maze. He finds them a wagon to ride in for the rest of their journey.

There are 6 things in the story above that are not true. Can you spot them?

Ask the student to read the text carefully and circle any false information that has been planted in the story.

This sheet can be cut or folded along the dotted line before presenting to the student.

- -

6 things that are not true:

The new baby dragons are not swimming in a stream. They do not see a hunter running across a bridge. The hunter does not knock Gold out of the sky with a ball. There is not a huge orange beast in the middle room. The beast does not whistle Gold a tune. The beast does not find them a wagon to ride in.

Book 6: Confusing Routes

Retelling the story

Use the story cards to sequence and tell the story.
Can be used as either an oral or a written activity. The teacher can choose whether to number any of cards 2 to 6.

Book 6: Confusing Routes

Picture the scene

Mina is on the left-hand side of the picture.

Purple and Green are eating from a sack of seeds at the front of the picture.

There is a brown dragon egg behind Mina.

In the background are two hills.

The ground is covered in grass and pebbles.

Ask the student to read the text carefully and draw the details of the picture as described in the text. Remind the student to read all the instructions through once before starting drawing.

Book 6: Confusing Routes

Dictation

Mina woke up feeling cold and in a bad __ ___ __.

"I wish I had a __ ___ ___ __ __ __ ___ and a big bottle of ___ __ __ __ ___," she grumbled.

Then an odd crunching and ___ ___ __ ___ noise distracted her. What was it?

Mina's bad __ ___ __ lifted when she saw the purple and golden eggs had both hatched.

The little dragons were ___ ___ __ ___ on the last of the __ ___ __.

Use the text at the bottom of the page for dictation. The section for dictation can either be cut off by the teacher or be folded along the dotted line to allow the student to self-check their spellings on completion. Dictate the passage to the student. Ask her/him to spell the missing words, writing a sound on each line. Explain that longer lines indicate spellings with more than one letter, e.g. t oo.

Mina woke up feeling cold and in a bad **m oo d**.

"I wish I had a **t oo th b r u sh** and a big bottle of **sh a m p oo**," she grumbled.

Then an odd crunching and **ch ew i ng** noise distracted her. What was it?

Mina's bad **m oo d** lifted when she saw the purple and golden eggs had both hatched.

The little dragons were **ch ew i ng** on the last of the **f oo d**.

Book 6: Confusing Routes

Developing vocabulary: **swooping**

The word 'swooping' is used here in Book 6:

> 'swooping' means: sweeping through the air like a bird

Circle the word or phrase that could be replaced with the word 'swooping' in the following text:

> It had taken Fabio twenty minutes to get the kite off the ground. The wind had it in its grip now, sending it sweeping through the air like a bird.

Can you write two different sentences of your own using the word 'swooping'?

1.

____

____

2.

____

____

Reading fluency

A shadow loomed over them. A gruesome beast shambled out of the gloom. He grabbed the hunter AND the blue egg! Then the beast reached out to stroke Gold's hurt wing. He began to croon.

"He's not a brute," said Mina softly. "He's singing to soothe Gold."

The blue beast chewed his lip. He was thinking. Then he handed Mina the blue egg.

"I think he trusts you," whispered Nat.

The hunter wriggled out of the beast's grip. He raced off back into the maze to find the rest of his crew.

The big, blue beast quickly led the group on a route out of the maze. The hunters were still lost inside!

Mina hugged the gentle beast. "Thanks for helping us get away from that foolish crew," she said with a grin.

Ask the student to read through the passage to familiarise themselves with the text.
Read it through for them again to model reading with expression and attention to punctuation.
Ask the student to read the passage again, thinking about adding expression to their reading and following punctuation in the passage. Students who struggle with punctuation may benefit from highlighting the punctuation in the text before reading.
Teachers can fold the page to cover the bottom paragraph of text to offer a shorter passage if needed.

Book 6: Confusing Routes

Make a page for a comic – reading comprehension

1

The purple and gold eggs have hatched overnight! The little dragons are eating all the food.

2

The group see a man with a blue egg going into a maze. They follow him, but get lost.

3

They spot a hot-air balloon in the sky. It's the hunters! The hunter's balloon crashes into the maze. Mina and Nat race to try and find the blue egg.

4

A big blue beast has caught the hunter AND the blue egg! He gives Mina the blue egg and helps the group find their way out of the maze.

Ask the student to read the text and draw a picture to match the text in each box.

Book 6: Confusing Routes

Dice game: words with 'oo' spellings

⚀ (1)	⚁ (2)	⚂ (3)	⚃ (4)	⚄ (5)	⚅ (6)
truth	boot	threw	super	cruel	flute
pool	rude	group	grew	blue	brutal
shoot	youth	true	rule	flew	judo
soothe	boon	brute	chew	July	glue
food	route	soup	scoop	clue	too

This game is for two players. Each player needs a batch of counters of one colour. The players take turns to throw the die. They read a word in the column that corresponds to the number on the die and place their counter on that word. The first to have three of her/his counters in a row in any direction is the winner.

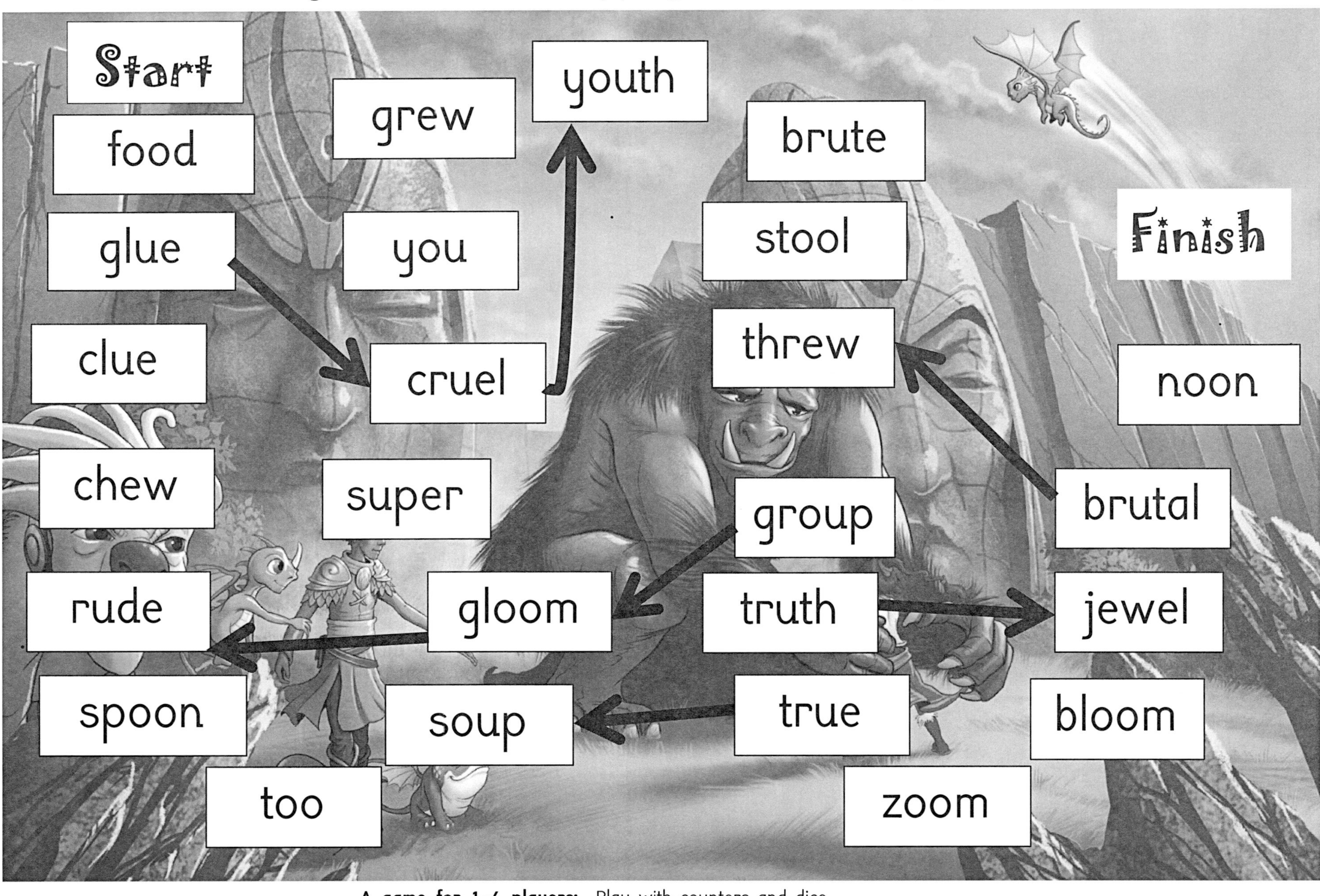

A game for 1–4 players: Play with counters and dice.
Players should read aloud the words that they land on at the end of each turn and follow the direction arrows if they land on them.

Book 6: Confusing Routes

Spelling assessment: words with 'oo' spellings

1.

oo	ou	ew	ue	u–e	u
too	you	grew	true	rude	truth
soon	soup	flew	blue	rule	July
cool	youth	drew	glue	brute	super

2.

oo	ou	ew	ue	u–e
swoop	group	chew	clueless	include
scoop	coupon	threw	cruel	conclude
foolish	route	screw	gruesome	delude

These lists can be used as a spelling assessment at the end of each book. The teacher can add words from list 2 for students who are ready for that stage. When dictating a word, first say the word on its own. Next, say a sentence with the word in it (to put the word in the context of a sentence) and then repeat the word. This ensures that the student has understood the word correctly, e.g. "Blue. The sky was a lovely bright blue. Blue."

Book 7: Finding the Light
Contents

Book 7: Finding the Light

Blending and segmenting: 'ie'

tie

light

fine

by

find

bright

drive

China

fries

shine

tonight

tried

Blend the sounds into a word. Segment the word into sounds by writing one sound in each square. Split vowel spellings (i–e) are represented by half squares linked together.

Book 7: Finding the Light

Reading and sorting words with 'ie' spellings

igh	ie	i-e	i	y

giant	idol	midnight	flies
knife	shine	mile	style
shy	thigh	slime	invite
final	try	mine	high
life	dried	kite	slight
find	line	why	pie
kind	dive	spies	nice
bright	lying	behind	fright

Photocopy this page onto card and cut out the words. Read and sort the cards out according to the 'ie' headings at the top of the page.

Book 7: Finding the Light

Reading and spelling words with 'ie' spellings

igh	ie	i-e
_______	_______	_______
_______	_______	_______
_______	_______	_______
_______	_______	_______

y	i
_______	_______
_______	_______
_______	_______
_______	_______

behind   final   try   high   bright   dried   kite   dive

why   spies   flies   shy   shine   lying   mine   slight

kind   midnight   pie   mind

List the words according to the 'ie' spellings.

Book 7: Finding the Light

Timed reading of words with 'ie' spellings

invite   spite   tonight   final   try   mine   high

life   dried   kite   slight   find   line   why   kind

nice   bright   behind   slime

1st try   Time:

---

invite   spite   tonight   final   try   mine   high

life   dried   kite   slight   find   line   why   kind

nice   bright   behind   slime

2nd try   Time:

---

invite   spite   tonight   final   try   mine   high

life   dried   kite   slight   find   line   why   kind

nice   bright   behind   slime

3rd try   Time:

This timed reading activity is for the student to improve her/his reading speed and fluency. Ask the student to read the words as fast as she/he can. Record the time in the box. Repeat the activity. This sheet can be cut or folded along the dotted lines to allow for different presentations.

Book 7: Finding the Light

Chunking two-syllable words with 'ie' spellings

sunlight	sun	light	sunlight
outside			
inside			
slimy			
magpie			
reply			
spicy			
dryer			
highlight			
decide			
denied			
bible			
rely			
delight			

Split the word into two syllables. Write each syllable in a box.
Write the whole word while saying the syllables. This worksheet allows the student to use the approach she/he has been taught for splitting words.

Book 7: Finding the Light
Syllable game 1

Die 1

Die 2

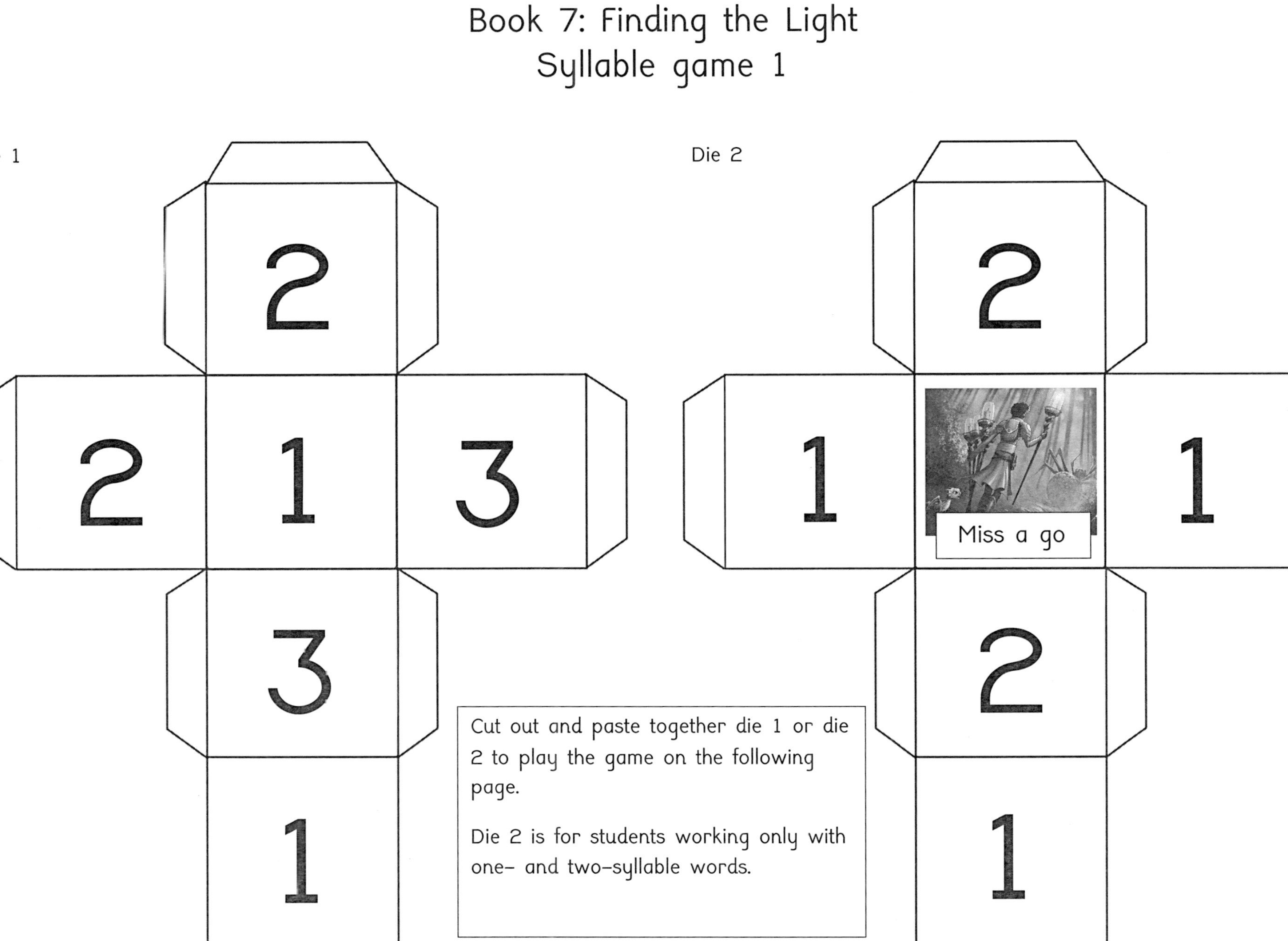

Cut out and paste together die 1 or die 2 to play the game on the following page.

Die 2 is for students working only with one- and two-syllable words.

Book 7: Finding the Light

Syllable game 2

sigh	midnight	delightful
try	magpie	spitefully
pie	spicy	highlighted
fine	twilight	frightening
bind	beside	bystander
fight	frying	decided

A game for 2 to 4 players

Photocopy this page onto card and cut the words out. Write the number of syllables in each word on the back of each card. For ease, the words have been arranged here in columns of one-, two- and three-syllable words. Use only the first two columns of cards for students working with just one- and two-syllable words. Turn the cards word-side up and mix up on a table.

Players take it in turns to roll the die and find a word that has the corresponding number of syllables. The player turns over the card they have selected to check they are right. If they are right, they keep the card. If not, the card is turned over again and remains in play.

Book 7: Finding the Light
Phonic patterns

Colour in the words with 'ie' spellings.

fright	truth	yelling	beside
youth	time	sunlight	towel
angry	finding	flew	crying
spiked	pine	midnight	fry
under	slight	kind	inside

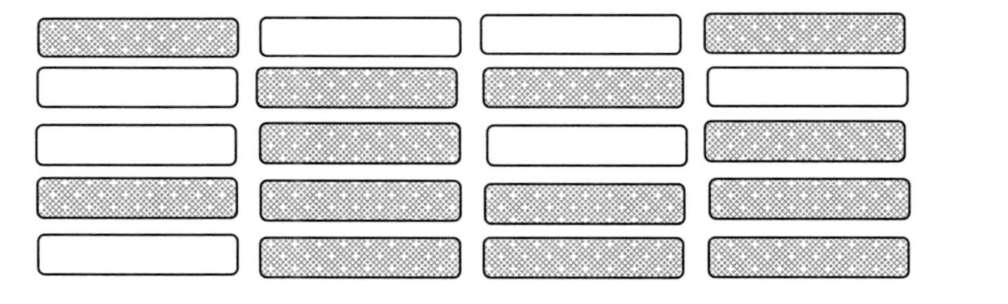

Fold this sheet along the dotted line. Read the words in the column on the left. Listen to the sounds in the words. Colour in the boxes with words that have 'ie' spellings. Repeat this with the other columns. Unfold the sheet and check that the correct words have been coloured in.
This sheet may be photocopied by the purchaser. © Phonic Books Ltd 2021

Book 7: Finding the Light

Is it true?

Mina wakes up to find Gold is playing hide and seek. She finds him inside a house at the top of the cliff. Nat meets a member of the pyrite tribe who invites him on a walk.

The pyrites have found an egg. They have hidden it in a box. The pyrites are frightened of a giant spider who comes out in the daylight. The hunters have stolen the pyrites' lights. Nat sets off to find the hunters and get the lights back.

Gold helps Nat sprinkle some cake crumbs in a giant spider web. The hunters try to get them and get stuck in the web. Nat uses a pair of scissors to cut the hunters out of the web. He lights a candle to scare the spider away.

The pyrites decide to keep the lilac egg.

There are 7 things in the story above that are not true. Can you spot them?

Ask the student to read the text carefully and circle any false information that has been planted in the story.
This sheet can be cut or folded along the dotted line before presenting to the student.

- -

7 things that are not true:
Gold is not hiding in a house. The pyrite does not invite Nat on a walk. The pyrites have not hidden the egg in a box. The giant spider does not come out in daylight. Gold and Nat do not sprinkle cake crumbs in the spider web. Nat does not use a pair of scissors to cut the web. The pyrites do not decide to keep the lilac egg.

Book 7: Finding the Light

Retelling the story

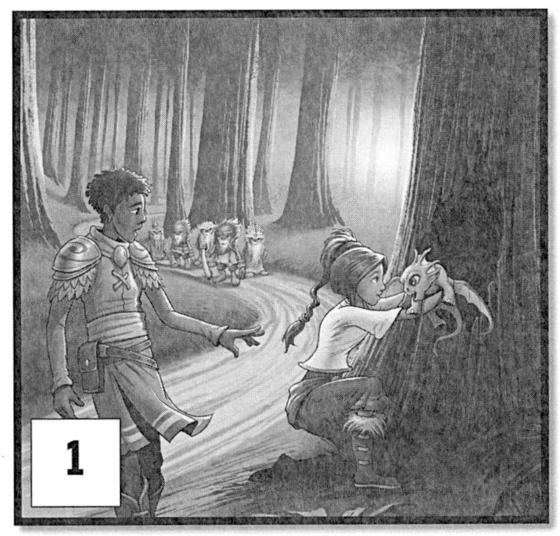

Use the story cards to sequence and tell the story.
Can be used as either an oral or a written activity. The teacher can choose whether to number any of cards 2 to 6.

This sheet may be photocopied by the purchaser. © Phonic Books Ltd 2021

Book 7: Finding the Light

Picture the scene

Four hunters are trapped in a giant spider's web.

The giant spider is in the top right-hand side of the picture.

Nat is in front of the web.

Gold is flying on the left-hand side of the picture.

There are trees around the edges of the picture.

Ask the student to read the text carefully and draw the details of the picture as described in the text. Remind the student to read all the instructions through once before starting drawing.

Book 7: Finding the Light

Dictation

The hunters escaped – running for their __ __ __ __ __!

The hunters were safe, but the __ __ __ __ ___ was still coming! He had __ __ ___ __ baby Gold!

The bag Mina had given Nat was filled with candles. Great for the __ ___ __ __! Nat topped each __ ___ __ with a candle from Mina's bag.

The candles were really __ __ ___ __.   The __ __ __ __ ___ hated that __ __ ___ __ __ ___ __! He retreated into the shadows.

This text is an adaptation of the text in Book 7. Use the text at the bottom of the page for dictation. The section for dictation can either be cut off by the teacher or be folded along the dotted line to allow the student to self-check their spellings on completion. Dictate the passage to the student. Ask her/him to spell the missing words, writing a sound on each line. Explain that longer lines indicate spellings with more than one letter e.g. **s** igh.

The hunters escaped – running for their **l i v e s**!

The hunters were safe, but the **s p i d er** was still coming! He had **s p ie d** baby Gold!

The bag Mina had given Nat was filled with candles. Great for the **l igh t s**! Nat topped each **l igh t** with a candle from Mina's bag.

The candles were really **b r igh t**. The **s p i d er** hated that **b r igh t l igh t**! He retreated into the shadows.

Book 7: Finding the Light

Developing vocabulary: **shreds**

The word 'shreds' is used here in Book 7:

> 'shreds' means: small pieces or scraps

Circle the word or phrase that could be replaced with the word 'shreds' in the following text:

> Dad had left a piece of paper in his pocket when he washed his shirt. When he opened the washing machine door, he found lots of tiny pieces of paper mixed in with the wet washing!

Can you write two different sentences of your own using the word 'shreds'?

1.

____

____

2.

____

____

Book 7: Finding the Light

Reading fluency

The group had been dozing in the shade. Mina woke up and stretched. A sudden squeak of delight made her look up. Gold had taken flight! He was playing hide and seek right at the top of a high cliff.

Mina sighed. "Why do you have to roam so much, Gold? You're a baby dragon, not a wild tiger."

She and Nat set off up the cliff to find the little dragon. They climbed up the knotted vines, trying not to slip as they left the ground way behind them.

They finally found Gold deep in the forest. He was hiding inside an old tree trunk in the forest.

"You drive me crazy, but I still like you," Mina said as she hugged him tight.

Ask the student to read through the passage to familiarise themselves with the text.
Read it through for them again to model reading with expression and attention to punctuation.
Ask the student to read the passage again, thinking about adding expression to their reading and following punctuation in the passage. Students who struggle with punctuation may benefit from highlighting the punctuation in the text before reading.
Teachers can fold the page to cover the bottom paragraph of text to offer a shorter passage if needed.

Book 7: Finding the Light

Make a page for a comic – reading comprehension

1

Gold is playing hide and seek! Nat and Mina finally find him inside a tree in the forest. A pyrite says hello and invites them to his camp.

2

They see the lilac egg hidden in a hut. The pyrites explain they are frightened of a giant spider who comes out at night. They use lights to keep him away.

3

The hunters have stolen the pyrites' lights. Nat sets off to find them. He traps the hunters in a giant spider web, but takes pity on them when the spider comes!

4

Nat chases the spider away with a candle that Mina has made. The pyrites give them the lilac egg and they set off again on their quest.

Ask the student to read the text and draw a picture to match the text in each box.

Book 7: Finding the Light

Dice game: words with 'ie' spellings

(1)	(2)	(3)	(4)	(5)	(6)
final	try	mine	high	life	dried
kite	slight	find	line	why	pie
kind	dive	spies	nine	bright	knife
shine	mile	style	giant	wife	tight
flies	shy	thigh	slime	invite	spite

This game is for two players. Each player needs a batch of counters of one colour. The players take turns to throw the die. They read a word in the column that corresponds to the number on the die and place their counter on that word. The first to have three of her/his counters in a row in any direction is the winner.

Start
sky
lime
my
high
kite
lie
try
spy
slimy
why
bike
fight
kind
fright
five
cried
final
shy
tight
hide
fried
Finish
my
drive
reply
China
strike

A game for 1–4 players: Play with counters and dice.
Players should read aloud the words that they land on at the end of each turn and follow the direction arrows if they land on them.

Book 7: Finding the Light

Spelling assessment: words with 'ie' spellings

1.

igh	ie	i-e	y	i
light	tie	time	my	find
might	lie	life	by	wild
tight	pie	ride	fly	final

2.

igh	ie	i-e	y	i
flight	cried	glide	frying	spider
fright	dried	smile	trying	giant
tonight	spied	stripe	crying	behind

These lists can be used as a spelling assessment at the end of each book. The teacher can add words from list 2 for students who are ready for that stage. When dictating a word, first say the word on its own. Next, say a sentence with the word in it (to put the word in the context of a sentence) and then repeat the word. This ensures that the student has understood the word correctly, e.g. "Smile. Seeing flowers always makes me smile. Smile."

Book 8: Falling Waters
Contents

Book 8: Falling Waters

Blending and segmenting: 'or'

Word				
saw	s	aw		
bore				
all				
war				
haunt				
brought				
talk				
torch				
before				
straw				
swarm				
small				

Blend the sounds into a word. Segment the word into sounds by writing one sound in each square.

Book 8: Falling Waters

Reading and sorting words with 'or' spellings

or	ore	a	ar	aw	au

al	ough	awe

fought	warm	awesome	halt
snore	sport	awful	walk
war	explore	stall	paw
talk	Autumn	claw	nought
stork	bore	almost	corn
haunt	swarm	thought	draw
born	tall	form	chalk

Photocopy this page onto card and cut out the words. Read and sort the cards out according to the 'or' headings at the top of the page.

Book 8: Falling Waters

Reading and spelling words with 'or' spellings

or	a	aw
_____	_____	_____
_____	_____	_____
_____	_____	_____
_____	_____	_____

al	ough
_____	_____
_____	_____
_____	_____

or   straw   call   claw   fought   for   small   all
halt   walk   thought   torch   draw   brought   stalk
sort   saw   talk

List the words according to the 'or' spellings.

Book 8: Falling Waters

Timed reading of words with 'or' spellings

or   straw   call   claw   fought   for   small   all   halt

walk   thought   torch   draw   brought   stalk   sort

saw   talk   sport

1st try   **Time:**

---

or   straw   call   claw   fought   for   small   all   halt

walk   thought   torch   draw   brought   stalk   sort

saw   talk   sport

2nd try   **Time:**

---

or   straw   call   claw   fought   for   small   all   halt

walk   thought   torch   draw   brought   stalk   sort

saw   talk   sport

3rd try   **Time:**

This timed reading activity is for the student to improve her/his reading speed and fluency. Ask the student to read the words as fast as she/he can. Record the time in the box. Repeat the activity. This sheet can be cut or folded along the dotted lines to allow for different presentations.

Book 8: Falling Waters

Chunking two-syllable words with 'or' spellings

report	re	port	report
shorten			
lawful			
awful			
morning			
before			
almost			
haunted			
warming			
thoughtful			
talking			
sorted			
boredom			
calling			

Split the word into two syllables. Write each syllable in a box.
Write the whole word while saying the syllables. This worksheet allows the student to use the
approach she/he has been taught for splitting words.

Book 8: Falling Waters
Syllable game 1

Die 1

Die 2

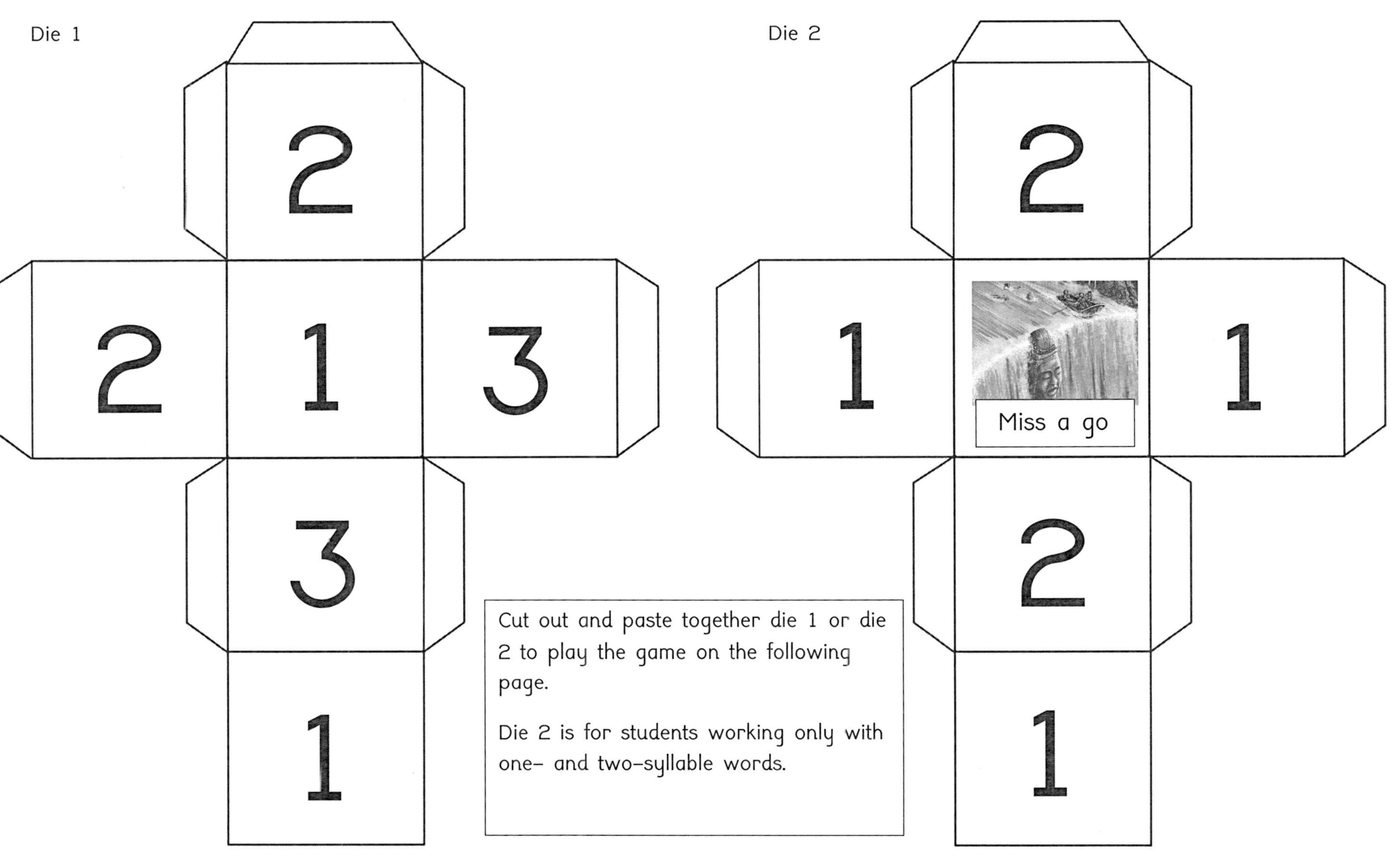

Cut out and paste together die 1 or die 2 to play the game on the following page.

Die 2 is for students working only with one- and two-syllable words.

Book 8: Falling Waters

Syllable game 2

paw	walkway	thoughtfully
sport	calling	reporter
tall	boredom	transported
talk	sorting	recalling
stall	awesome	exporting
born	haunted	freefalling

A game for 2 to 4 players

Photocopy this page onto card and cut the words out. Write the number of syllables in each word on the back of each card. For ease, the words have been arranged here in columns of one-, two- and three-syllable words. Use only the first two columns of cards for students working with just one- and two-syllable words. Turn the cards word-side up and mix up on a table.

Players take it in turns to roll the die and find a word that has the corresponding number of syllables. The player turns over the card they have selected to check they are right. If they are right, they keep the card. If not, the card is turned over again and remains in play.

Book 8: Falling Waters

Phonic patterns

Colour in the words with 'or' spellings.

born	torch	blue	brought
youth	carton	straw	warning
ball	explore	walkway	button
awesome	sport	talk	morning
under	farmer	mutter	August

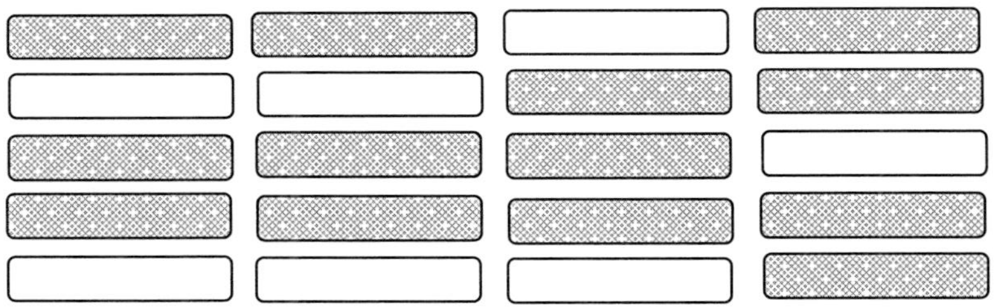

Fold this sheet along the dotted line. Read the words in the column on the left. Listen to the sounds in the words. Colour in the boxes with words that have 'or' spellings. Repeat this with the other columns. Unfold the sheet and check that the correct words have been coloured in.

Book 8: Falling Waters

Is it true?

The search for the next egg begins. Nat is worried that the baby dragons are thirsty. Mina is looking up at the sun and stumbles. She falls down a trail of steps and lands awkwardly in a spiky bush.

The silver egg rolls off Bain's back and splashes into the river! Mina jumps in to try and save it, but bumps her head on a rock. Mina is swept along by the current. Suddenly a blue baby dragon pops up beside her!

A swarm of bounty hunters hurtles past them. They are chasing a red egg. Blue tips the hunter's raft from underneath and they almost fall in the water. The raft tumbles over the edge of a waterfall! Mina almost falls over too, but luckily Nat leans into the water and pulls her to safety!

Nat is happy Mina is safe, but he feels bad about losing Blue. At the last minute, Blue flies up out of the water. She has a dragon egg in her mouth!

There are 7 things in the story above that are not true. Can you spot them?

Ask the student to read the text carefully and circle any false information that has been planted in the story.

This sheet can be cut or folded along the dotted line before presenting to the student.

- -

7 things that are not true:
Nat is not worried that the baby dragons are thirsty. Mina is not looking up at the sun. Mina does not land in a spiky bush. The silver egg does not roll off Bain's back. Mina does not bump her head on a rock. Nat does not pull Mina to safety. Blue does not have a dragon egg in her mouth.

Book 8: Falling Waters

Retelling the story

Use the story cards to sequence and tell the story.
Can be used as either an oral or a written activity. The teacher can choose whether to number any of cards 2 to 6.

Book 8: Falling Waters

Picture the scene

A wide river flows down the middle of the picture, from the top to bottom of the picture.

There are grassy banks along both sides of the river.

Mina is floating on her back in the river.

The little dragon, Blue, is floating next to Mina.

Blue's egg shells are floating in the water behind them.

Ask the student to read the text carefully and draw the details of the picture as described in the text. Remind the student to read all the instructions through once before starting drawing.

Book 8: Falling Waters

Dictation

Mina and Nat had ___ __ ____ __ __ asleep curled up in a heap with the baby dragons. __ ____ __ was breaking as they woke up. Mina __ ____ __ ____ and stretched.

"Ready __ ____ the __ ____ __ __ ____ to start?" teased Nat. They set off to search for the next egg. Mina __ ____ ____ over the gem, willing it to glow. She was so __ __ __ ____ __ ____ that she __ ____ __ ____ way off the track.

Bain __ ____ __ ____ close by, keeping her safe.

Use the text at the bottom of the page for dictation. The section for dictation can either be cut off by the teacher or be folded along the dotted line to allow the student to self-check their spellings on completion. Dictate the passage to the student. Ask her/him to spell the missing words, writing a sound on each line. Explain that longer lines indicate spellings with more than one letter, e.g. s aw.

Mina and Nat had **f a ll e n** asleep curled up in a heap with the baby dragons. **D aw n** was breaking as they woke up. Mina **y aw n ed** and stretched.

"Ready **f or** the **m or n i ng** to start?" teased Nat.

They set off to search for the next egg. Mina **p or ed** over the gem, willing it to glow. She was so **a b s or b ed** that she **w al k ed** way off the track.

Bain **w al k ed** close by, keeping her safe.

Book 8: Falling Waters

Developing vocabulary: **pored over**

The words 'pored over' are used here in Book 8:

'pored over' means: looked at with great attention

Circle the word or phrase that could be replaced with the words 'pored over' in the following text:

"I'm sure that's you, third from the right," said Mum as she stared at the old school photo on Grandad's bedroom wall.

Can you write two different sentences of your own using the words 'pored over'?

1.

____

____

2.

____

____

Book 8: Falling Waters

Reading fluency

Mina had landed next to a river. Her arm was sore from her fall. Bain charged forward, trying to help her. The blue egg rolled off his back as he ran. It bounced down the steps… and right into the water!

"We must get that egg!" yelled Mina.

There was no time to pause and think. She launched herself off the river bank and into the water. Mina was a strong swimmer, but the current was even stronger. She began to struggle.

Nat saw a bridge that crossed over the river. Mina was almost underneath it. He grabbed a branch and ran onto the bridge.

"Grab this, Mina!" he yelled.

Mina reached up, but the branch was too short.

Ask the student to read through the passage to familiarise themselves with the text.
Read it through for them again to model reading with expression and attention to punctuation.
Ask the student to read the passage again, thinking about adding expression to their reading and following punctuation in the passage. Students who struggle with punctuation may benefit from highlighting the punctuation in the text before reading.
Teachers can fold the page to cover the bottom paragraph of text to offer a shorter passage if needed.

Book 8: Falling Waters

Make a page for a comic – reading comprehension

1

They set off to search for the next egg. Mina is poring over the gem, and trips. She falls down a trail of rocky steps! Her arm is sore.

2

Bain runs to help her. The blue egg rolls off his back and falls into the river. Mina jumps into the water to try and save it.

3

Mina floats down the river in the current. The blue egg hatches into a tiny blue dragon! A raft full of hunters floats past, chasing an orange egg.

4

The raft falls over a waterfall! Bain pulls Mina to safety. They have lost the blue dragon. The blue dragon pops up out of the water, holding the orange egg!

Ask the student to read the text and draw a picture to match the text in each box.

Book 8: Falling Waters

Dice game: words with 'or' spellings

(1)	(2)	(3)	(4)	(5)	(6)
corn	bore	warn	talk	all	paw
warm	fought	port	draw	torch	raw
small	war	stalk	store	maul	call
sore	saw	haunt	fall	short	more
crawl	sport	snore	August	hall	ball

This game is for two players. Each player needs a batch of counters of one colour. The players take turns to throw the die. They read a word in the column that corresponds to the number on the die and place their counter on that word. The first to have three of her/his counters in a row in any direction is the winner.

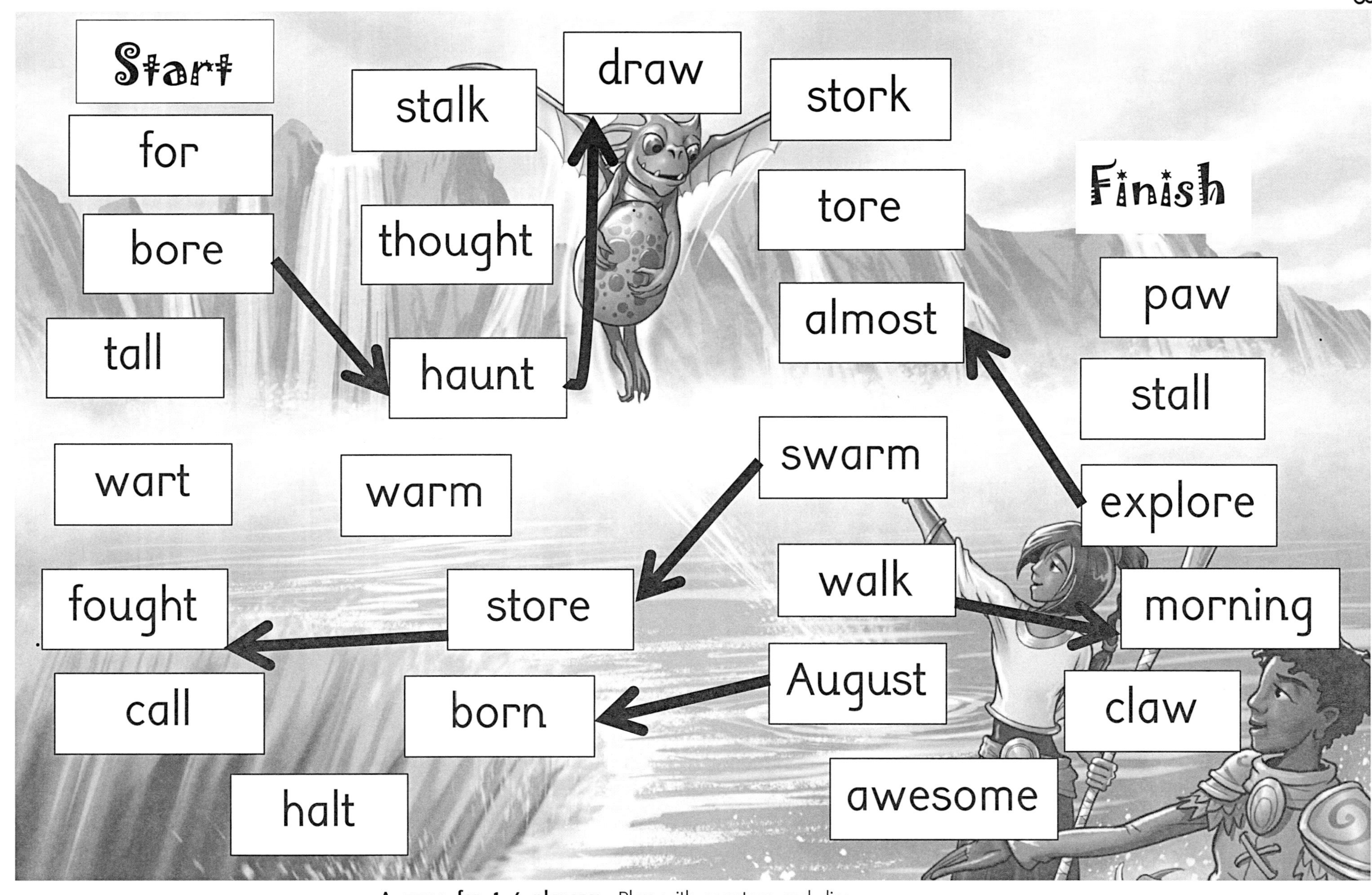

A game for 1–4 players: Play with counters and dice.
Players should read aloud the words that they land on at the end of each turn and follow the direction arrows if they land on them.

Book 8: Falling Waters

Spelling assessment: words with 'or' spellings

or	ore	aw	au	a
for	more	saw	maul	all
sort	sore	claw	haunt	call
torch	store	draw	August	almost

ar	awe	al	ough
warm	awe	walk	fought
swarm	awesome	talk	thought

These lists can be used as a speling assessment at the end of each book. The teacher may want to offer this test in two halves as there are so many words. When dictating a word, first say the word on its own. Next, say a sentence with the word in it (to put the word in the context of a sentence) and then repeat the word. This ensures that the student has understood the word correctly, e.g. "Warm. It was lovely and warm sitting in the sun. Warm."

Book 9: A Daring Raid
Contents

Book 9: A Daring Raid

Blending and segmenting: 'air'

hair	h	air				
dare						
their						
chair						
pear						
where						
spare						
stair						
beware						
careless						
impaired						
werewolf						

Blend the sounds into a word. Segment the word into sounds by writing one sound in each square.

Book 9: A Daring Raid

Reading and sorting words with 'air' spellings

air	**are**	**ear**	**ere**	**eir**

hare	glare	pairs	fairly
fare	chair	rare	swear
heir	lair	stare	bear
mare	flair	tear	dare
where	their	bare	pear
spare	affair	fair	declare
despair	care	stare	impair
pair	blare	wear	there

Photocopy this page onto card and cut out the words. Read and sort the cards out according to the 'air' headings at the top of the page.

Book 9: A Daring Raid

Reading and spelling words with 'air' spellings

air	are	ear
___________	___________	___________
___________	___________	___________
___________	___________	___________
___________	___________	___________
___________	___________	___________

ere	eir
___________	___________
___________	

where	air	bear	there	their	fair	chair	dare
pear	share	tear	stair	glare	spare	wear	swear
despair	bare						

List the words according to the 'air' spellings.

Book 9: A Daring Raid

Timed reading of words with 'air' spellings

hairy   rare   air   there   pear   chair   care

where   flare   their   wear   stare   fair   beware

scare   despair   rare   bear   share

1st try   Time:

----

hairy   rare   air   there   pear   chair   care

where   flare   their   wear   stare   fair   beware

scare   despair   rare   bear   share

2nd try   Time:

----

hairy   rare   air   there   pear   chair   care

where   flare   their   wear   stare   fair   beware

scare   despair   rare   bear   share

3rd try   Time:

This timed reading activity is for the student to improve her/his reading speed and fluency. Ask the student to read the words as fast as she/he can. Record the time in the box. Repeat the activity. This sheet can be cut or folded along the dotted lines to allow for different presentations.

Book 9: A Daring Raid

Chunking two-syllable words with 'air' spellings

Word	Syllable 1	Syllable 2	Whole word
unfair	un	fair	unfair
footwear			
beware			
fairly			
nowhere			
farewell			
despair			
affair			
careless			
rarely			
heirloom			
hairless			
repair			
declare			

Split the word into two syllables. Write each syllable in a box.
Write the whole word while saying the syllables. This worksheet allows the student to use the approach she/he has been taught for splitting 'words.

Book 9: A Daring Raid
Syllable game 1

Die 1

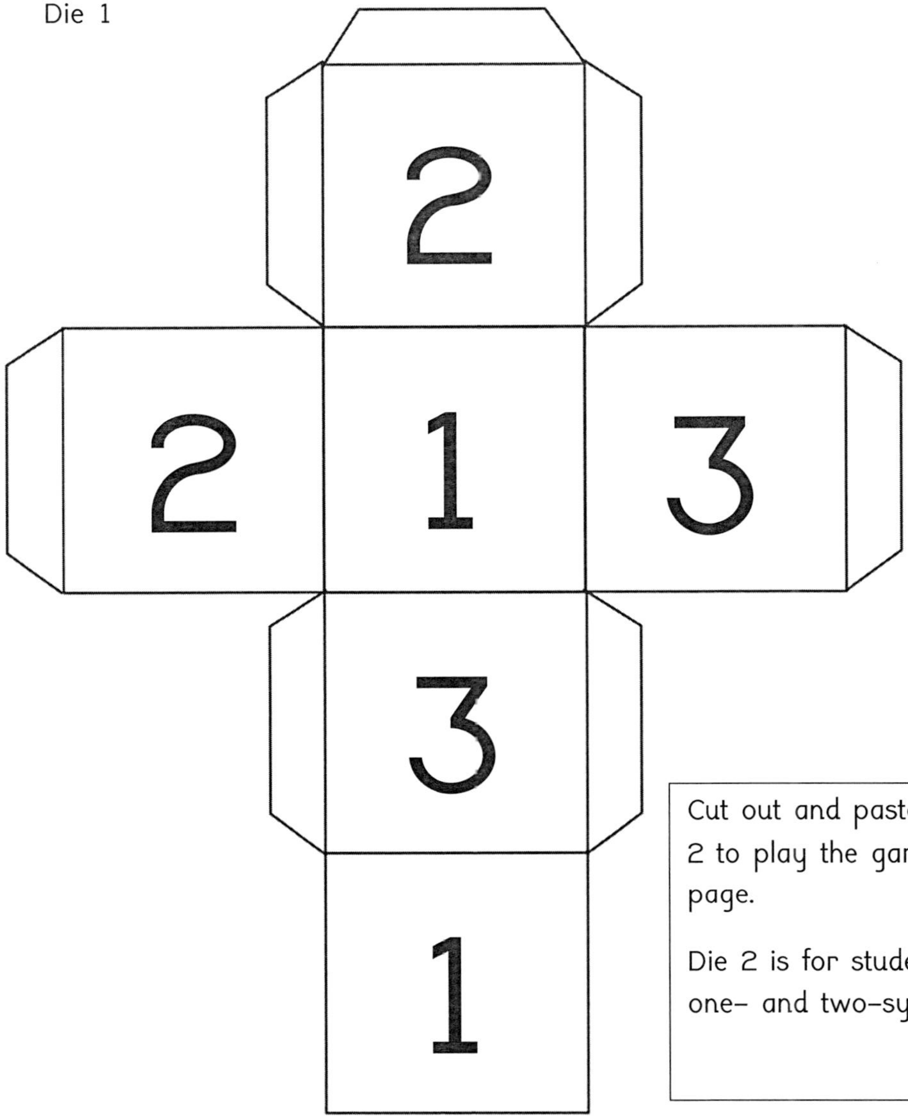

2

2 1 3

3

1

Die 2

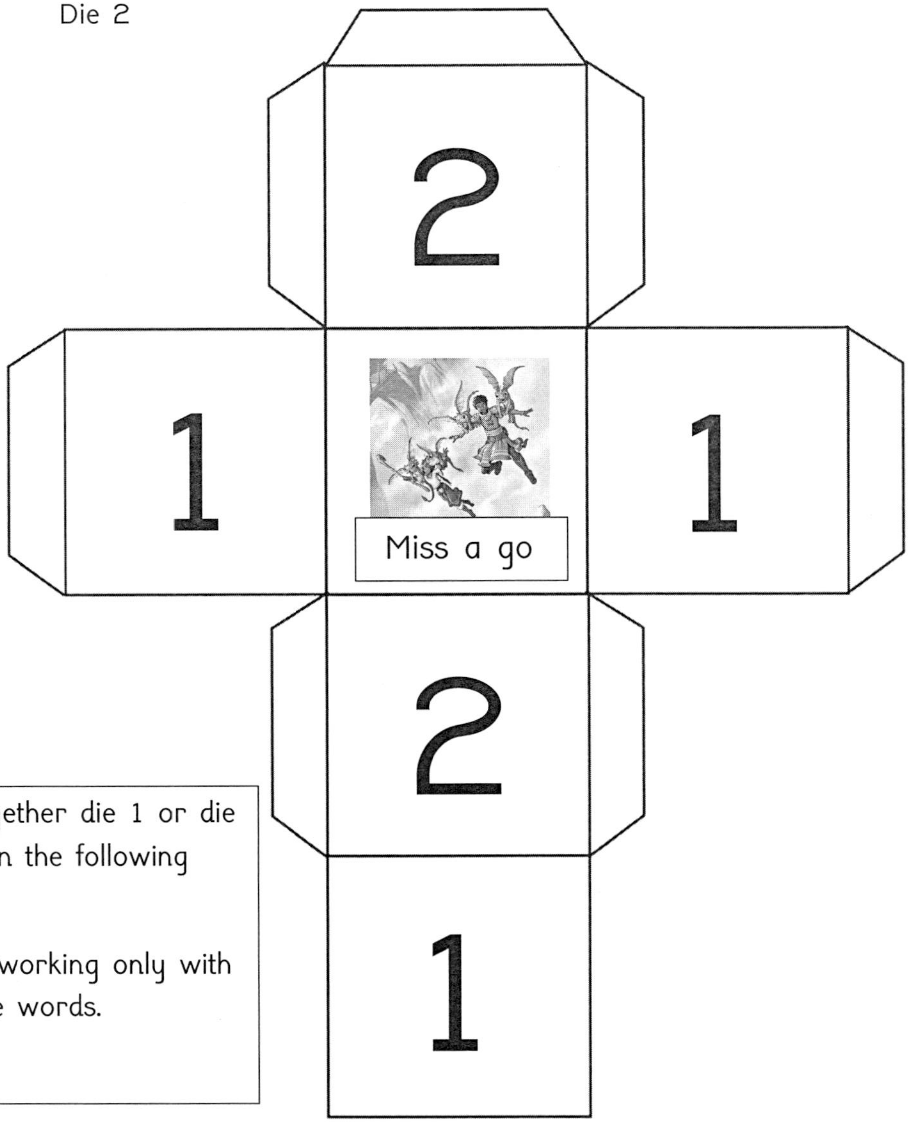

2

1 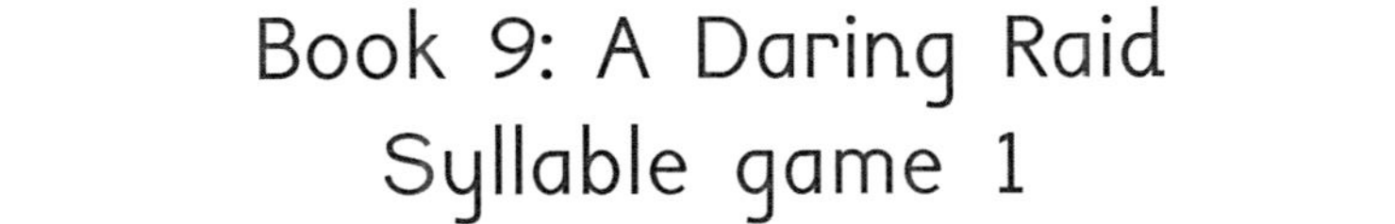
Miss a go
1

2

1

Cut out and paste together die 1 or die 2 to play the game on the following page.

Die 2 is for students working only with one- and two-syllable words.

Book 9: A Daring Raid

Syllable game 2

share	stairway	carefully
chair	beware	repairing
pear	careless	unfairly
their	nowhere	despairing
where	footwear	whereabouts
fair	farewell	underwear

A game for 2 to 4 players

Photocopy this page onto card and cut the words out. Write the number of syllables in each word on the back of each card. For ease, the words have been arranged here in columns of one-, two- and three-syllable words. Use only the first two columns of cards for students working with just one- and two-syllable words. Turn the cards word-side up and mix up on a table.

Players take it in turns to roll the die and find a word that has the corresponding number of syllables. The player turns over the card they have selected to check they are right. If they are right, they keep the card. If not, the card is turned over again and remains in play.

Book 9: A Daring Raid

Phonic patterns

Colour in the words with 'air' spellings.

stain	fair	nail	spare
where	great	unfair	despair
care	statement	bear	trade
tray	their	claim	swear
stairs	pear	dare	there

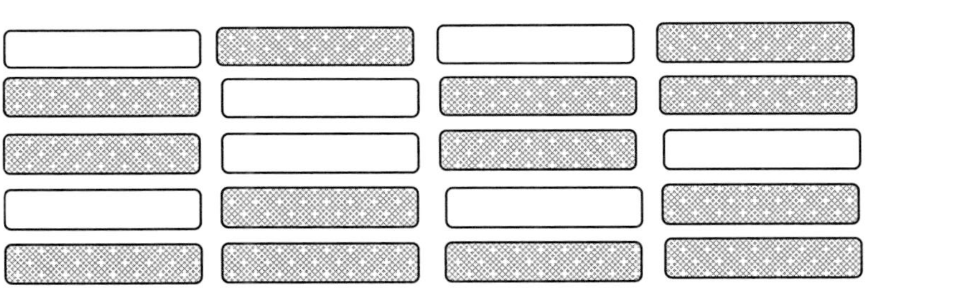

Fold this sheet along the dotted line. Read the words in the column on the left. Listen to the sounds in the words. Colour in the boxes with words that have 'air' spellings. Repeat this with the other columns. Unfold the sheet and check that the correct words have been coloured in.

Book 9: A Daring Raid

Is it true?

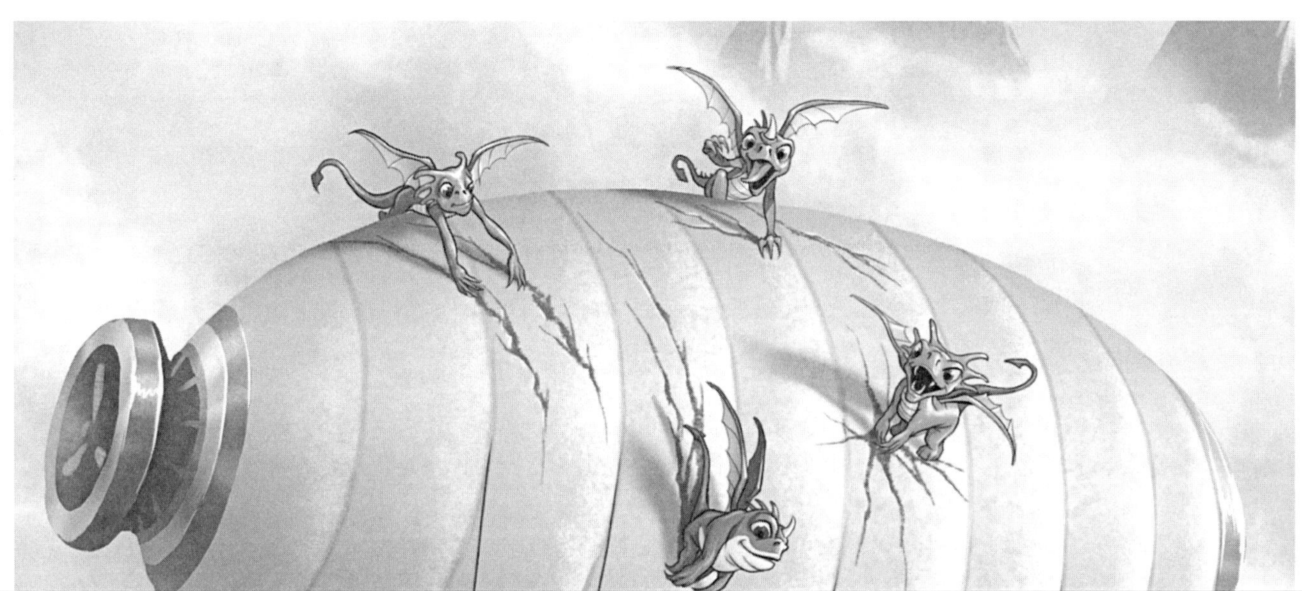

Mina spots a string of shapes hidden in the sky. What is it? She thinks it is an airship. She sees a family of bears up there! Nat explains it is a pair of mountains. A red egg is trapped up there. They need to get there. The baby dragons carry them up to the mountains by holding onto their hair. The hunters arrive on the island, hanging onto kites. Blue bursts the balloon on the airship with her claws. The hunters hide in the cave. Nat and Green make a snare from the bear's old hair. They trap the bear. Mina rescues the red dragon from the cave. She lowers him down to Bain in a basket.

There are 8 things in the story above that are not true. Can you spot them?

Ask the student to read the text carefully and circle any false information that has been planted in the story.

This sheet can be cut or folded along the dotted line before presenting to the student.

- -

8 things that are not true:
Mina does not think the shapes are an airship. Mina does not see a family of bears up there. There is not a red egg trapped up there. The baby dragons do not hold onto Nat and Mina by their hair. The hunters are not hanging onto kites. The hunters do not hide in the cave. Nat and Green do not make a snare from the bear's old hair. Mina does not lower the red dragon down in a basket.

Book 9: A Daring Raid

Retelling the story

Use the story cards to sequence and tell the story.
Can be used as either an oral or a written activity. The teacher can choose whether to number any of cards 2 to 6.

Book 9: A Daring Raid

Picture the scene

There is a hot-air balloon shaped like an egg in the middle of the picture.

There is a basket hanging underneath the balloon.

There are three hunters in the basket.

Four baby dragons are on top of the balloon.

There are clouds all around the balloon.

Ask the student to read the text carefully and draw the details of the picture as described in the text. Remind the student to read all the instructions through once before starting drawing.

Book 9: A Daring Raid

Dictation

Gold had taken to the ___, flying high over the rest of them. Suddenly he began to squawk and flap his wings.

"___ ___ are you looking?" asked Nat, puzzled.

"___ ___' _ nothing up ___ ___."

But Gold was still looking up. Suddenly Mina was

_ _ ___ of a string of shapes high up above them. They were standing under a _ ___ of floating islands!

Mina spotted a _ ___ sight. A massive, _ ___ _

_ ___ sat on one of the islands.

Use the text at the bottom of the page for dictation. The section for dictation can either be cut off by the teacher or be folded along the dotted line to allow the student to self-check their spellings on completion. Dictate the passage to the student. Ask her/him to spell the missing words, writing a sound on each line. Explain that longer lines indicate spellings with more than one letter ,e.g. h air.

Gold had taken to the **air**, flying high over the rest of them. Suddenly he began to squawk and flap his wings.
"**Wh ere** are you looking?" asked Nat, puzzled. "**Th ere 's** nothing up **th ere**,"
But Gold was still looking up. Suddenly Mina was **a w are** of a string of shapes high up above them. They were standing under a **p air** of floating islands!
Mina spotted a **r are** sight. A massive, **h air y b ear** sat on one of the islands.

Book 9: A Daring Raid

Developing vocabulary: **clambered**

The word 'clambered' is used here in Book 9:

'clambered' means: climbed using hands and feet

Circle the word or phrase that could be replaced with the word 'clambered' in the following text:

The cat had seen the dog coming. She did not want him to get any closer. She raced up the fence as quick as a flash.

Can you write two different sentences of your own using the word 'clambered'?

1.

____

____

2.

____

____

Book 9: A Daring Raid

Reading fluency

It was time to get going. Mina stared at the gem.

"Where will you take us this time?" she asked it.

The glare of the sun made it hard to see if the gem was glowing.

She rubbed it. It seemed to be turning red.

Gold had taken to the air, flying high over the rest of them.

Suddenly he began to squawk and flap his wings.

"Where are you looking?" asked Nat, puzzled. "There's nothing up

there."

Gold was still looking up. Suddenly Mina was aware of a string of

shapes high up above them. The shapes were hidden in the

clouds. She gasped. They were standing under a pair of floating

islands!

Ask the student to read through the passage to familiarise themselves with the text.
Read it through for them again to model reading with expression and attention to punctuation.
Ask the student to read the passage again, thinking about adding expression to their reading and following
punctuation in the passage. Students who struggle with punctuation may benefit from highlighting the
punctuation in the text before reading.
Teachers can fold the page to cover the bottom paragraph of text to offer a shorter passage if needed.

Book 9: A Daring Raid

Make a page for a comic – reading comprehension

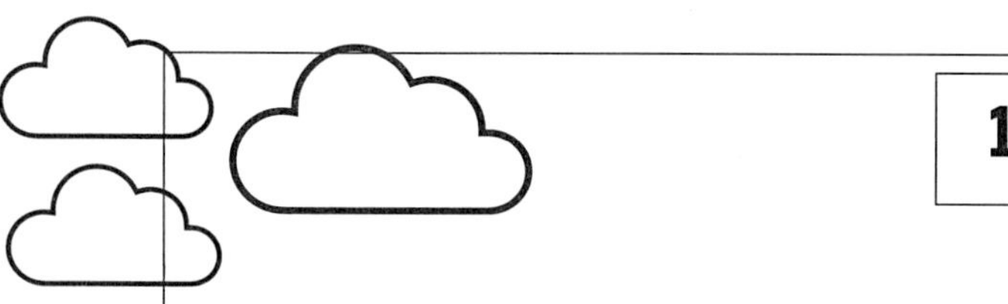

1

The gem is glowing red. Gold takes to the skies and seems to be staring at something. What has he seen? Mina spots a pair of islands floating in the sky!

2

The islands are really mountains. Mina sees a massive bear and a tiny red dragon trapped in his lair. The baby dragons fly Mina and Nat up to the mountains.

3

The hunters try to get to the red dragon in a hot-air balloon. The baby dragons land on the top of the balloon and tear holes in it with their claws.

4

Nat and Green make a snare with knotted ropes. They climb a tree and use the snare to trap the bear. Mina lowers Red down the mountain in a rope swing.

Ask the student to read the text and draw a picture to match the text in each box.

Book 9: A Daring Raid

Dice game: words with 'air' spellings

1	2	3	4	5	6
glare	dairy	rare	hairy	air	dare
there	heir	pear	chair	care	where
flare	wear	their	stairs	fair	spare
share	stare	fairly	bear	careful	bare
snare	mare	affair	tear	hair	hare

This game is for two players. Each player needs a batch of counters of one colour. The players take turns to throw the die. They read a word in the column that corresponds to the number on the die and place their counter on that word. The first to have three of her/his counters in a row in any direction is the winner.

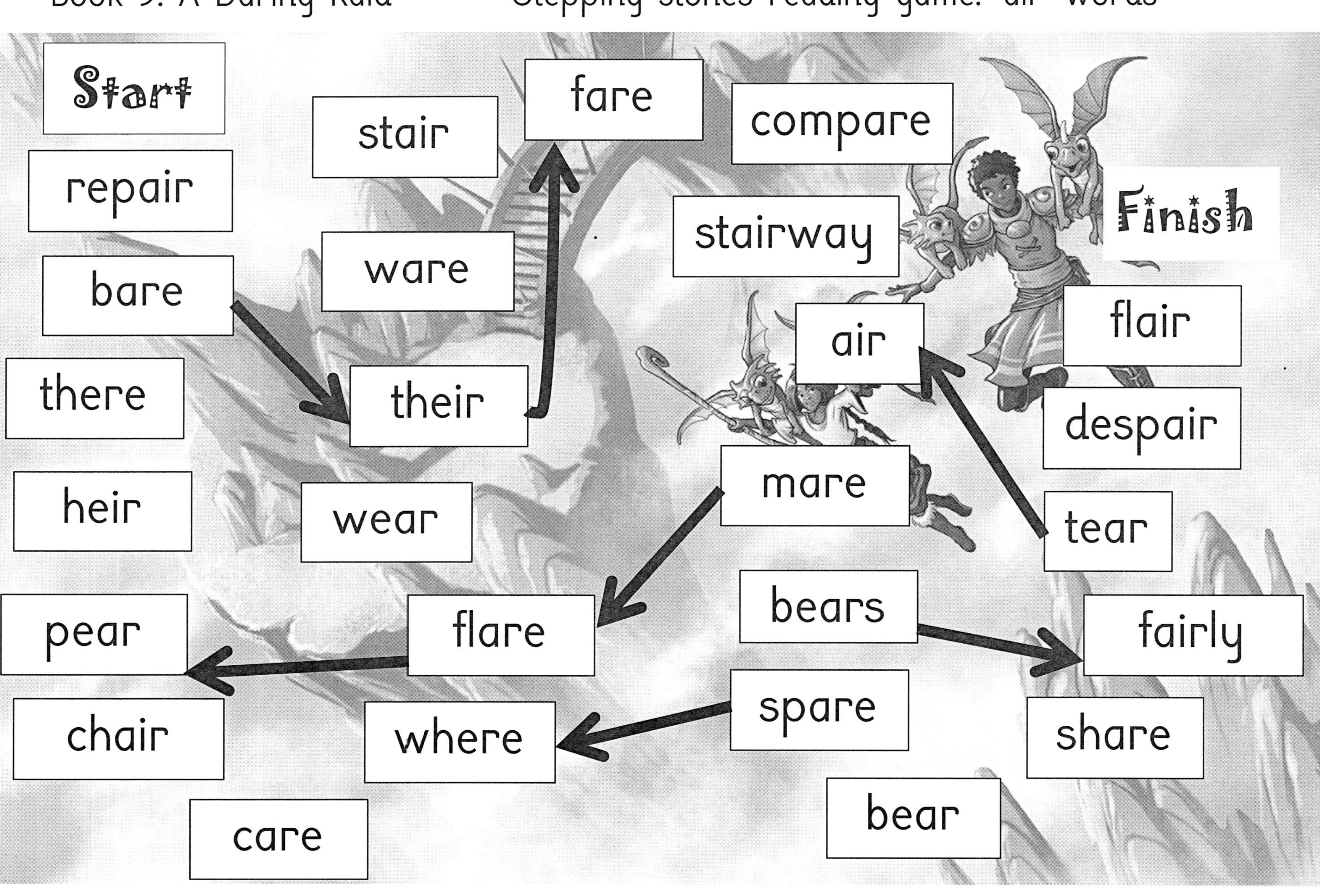

A game for 1–4 players: Play with counters and dice.
Players should read aloud the words that they land on at the end of each turn and follow the direction arrows if they land on them.

Book 9: A Daring Raid

Spelling assessment: words with 'air' spellings

1.

air	are	ear	ere	eir
fair	bare	bear	there	their
chair	dare	pear	where	
stair	share	tear		

2.

air	are	ear
repair	glare	swear
unfair	compare	wearing
	unaware	unbearable

These lists can be used as a spelling assessment at the end of each book. The teacher can add words from list 2 for students who are ready for that stage. When dictating a word, first say the word on its own. Next, say a sentence with the word in it (to put the word in the context of a sentence) and then repeat the word. This ensures that the student has understood the word correctly, e.g. "Chair. The cat was curled up asleep on the chair. Chair."

Book 10: Breaking the Charm
Contents

Book 10: Breaking the Charm

Blending and segmenting: 'ar'

art	ar	t			
ask					
half					
laugh					
heart					
path					
hard					
calm					
shark					
alarm					
hearth					
faster					

Blend the sounds into a word. Segment the word into sounds by writing one sound in each square.

Book 10: Breaking the Charm

Reading and sorting words with 'ar' spellings

ar	a	au	ear	al

sharp	hearth	shard	charm
almond	castle	last	yard
harsh	ask	laugh	raft
past	shark	palm	heart
faster	half	calm	harm
after	star	dark	draught
trance	aunt	dance	calf
bark	cast	army	march

Photocopy this page onto card and cut out the words. Read and sort the cards out according to the 'ar' headings at the top of the page.

Book 10: Breaking the Charm

Reading and spelling words with 'ar' spellings

al	a	ar
_______	_______	_______
_______	_______	_______
_______	_______	_______
_______	_______	_______
	_______	_______

ear	au
_______	_______
_______	_______

fast   car   palm   heart   laugh   ask   art   calm

hearth   draught   path   half   master   calf   farm   father

plaster   shark   alarm   almond   park

List the words according to the 'ar' spellings.

Book 10: Breaking the Charm

Timed reading of words with 'ar' spellings

craft	last	harm	palm	laugh	mark	heart
mask	shark	alarm	starve	half	blast	clasp
	aunt	cart	park	path	dance	

1st try   **Time:**

---

craft	last	harm	palm	laugh	mark	heart
mask	shark	alarm	starve	half	blast	clasp
	aunt	cart	park	path	dance	

2nd try   **Time:**

---

craft	last	harm	palm	laugh	mark	heart
mask	shark	alarm	starve	half	blast	clasp
	aunt	cart	park	path	dance	

3rd try   **Time:**

This timed reading activity is for the student to improve her/his reading speed and fluency. Ask the student to read the words as fast as she/he can. Record the time in the box. Repeat the activity. This sheet can be cut or folded along the dotted lines to allow for different presentations.

Book 10: Breaking the Charm

Chunking two-syllable words with 'ar' spellings

harmful	harm	ful	harmful
artist			
basket			
father			
laughter			
hearty			
plaster			
advance			
castle			
darkness			
almond			
draughty			
craftsman			
parchment			

Split the word into two syllables. Write each syllable in a box.
Write the whole word while saying the syllables. This worksheet allows the student to use the approach she/he has been taught for splitting words.

Book 10: Breaking the Charm
Syllable game 1

Die 1

Die 2

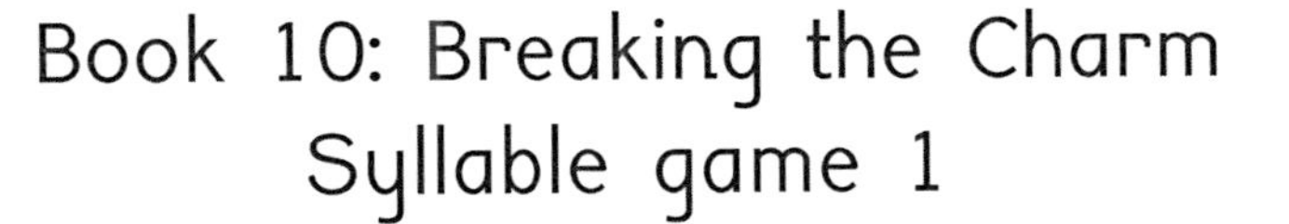

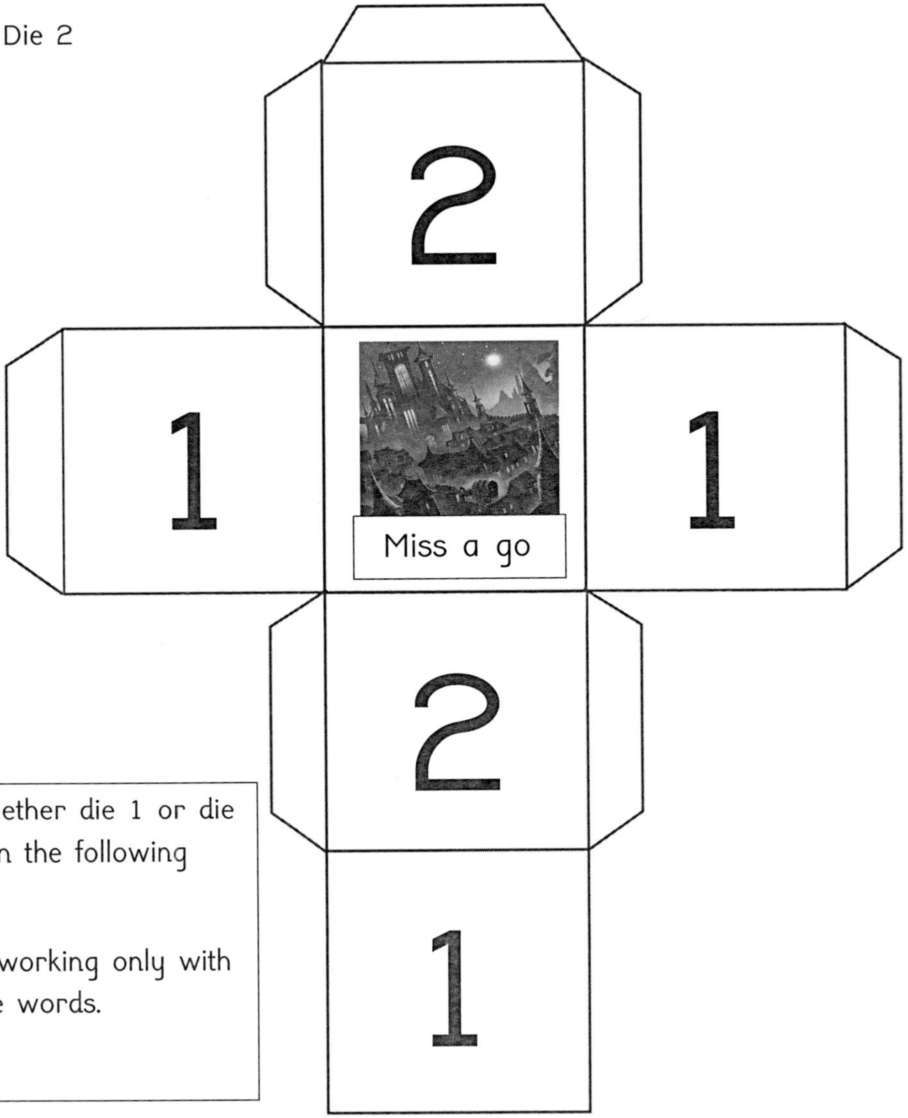

Cut out and paste together die 1 or die 2 to play the game on the following page.

Die 2 is for students working only with one- and two-syllable words.

Book 10: Breaking the Charm

Syllable game 2

sharp	artist	plastering
calm	darkness	fatherly
path	carton	sharpener
shark	starving	marketing
dance	sparkle	fastener
aunt	father	halfhearted

A game for 2 to 4 players

Photocopy this page onto card and cut the words out. Write the number of syllables in each word on the back of each card. For ease, the words have been arranged here in columns of one-, two- and three-syllable words. Use only the first two columns of cards for students working with just one- and two-syllable words. Turn the cards word-side up and mix up on a table.

Players take it in turns to roll the die and find a word that has the corresponding number of syllables. The player turns over the card they have selected to check they are right. If they are right, they keep the card. If not, the card is turned over again and remains in play.

Book 10: Breaking the Charm
Phonic patterns

Colour in the words with 'ar' spellings.

task	laughter	splash	spare
shark	planning	start	aunt
half	strain	trade	carpark
shape	class	flask	starting
standing	heart	nasty	alarm

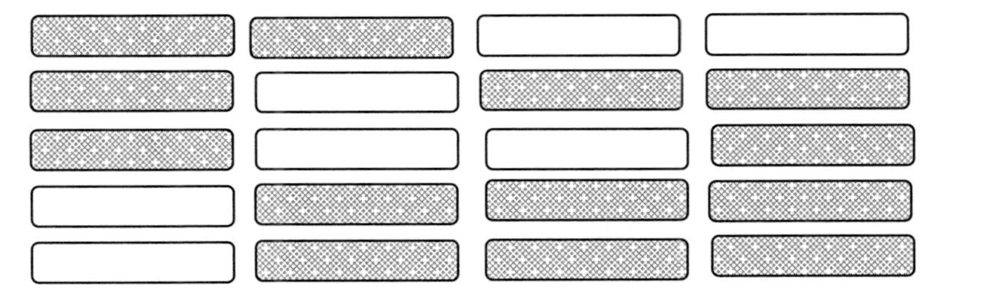

Fold this sheet along the dotted line. Read the words in the column on the left. Listen to the sounds in the words. Colour in the lozenges with words that have 'ar' spellings. Repeat this with the other columns. Unfold the sheet and check that the correct words have been coloured in.

Book 10: Breaking the Charm

Is it true?

There is one last dragon egg to find. Mina asks an artist if he has seen it. Mina and Nat realise the hunters work for the collector. They smuggle into the collector's castle in the back of a cart filled with cans of fish. It is almost morning when they arrive at the castle. The baby dragons are all asleep in the cart.

They break into the castle and set off the alarm. The collector holds up a large candle that acts like a charm and puts everyone in a trance. Mina knocks over a large jug and smashes it.

Nat finds a big machine. There is a huge clock at the centre of it. He breaks the machine with a wrench.

Bella the dragon appears and the family are reunited at last!

> There are 7 things in the story above that are not true. Can you spot them?

Ask the student to read the text carefully and circle any false information that has been planted in the story.

This sheet can be cut or folded along the dotted line before presenting to the student.

- -

7 things that are not true:
Mina does not ask an artist about the egg. The cart is not filled with cans of fish. It is not almost morning when they arrive at the castle. The baby dragons are not all asleep in the cart. The collector does not hold up a large candle. Mina does not knock over a jug. There is not a huge clock at the centre of the machine.

Book 10: Breaking the Charm

Retelling the story

1

Use the story cards to sequence and tell the story.
Can be used as either an oral or a written activity. The teacher can choose whether to number any of cards 2 to 6.

Book 10: Breaking the Charm

Picture the scene

The collector is standing at the back of the picture.

He is at the top of a flight of stairs.

He has a charm swinging from one hand.

Three baby dragons are asleep on the floor in front of him.

Nat is at the left-hand side of the picture.

Ask the student to read the text carefully and draw the details of the picture as described in the text. Remind the student to read all the instructions through once before starting drawing.
This sheet may be photocopied by the purchaser. © Phonic Books Ltd 2021

Book 10: Breaking the Charm

Dictation

The __ ____ __ ____ had a plan to help them. He pointed to the back of his __ ____ __.

The __ ____ __ was loaded with __ __ __ __ __ __ __ __ of salt. They all hid in the back of the __ ____ __ as the __ ____ __ ____ drove the salt up to the __ __ ____ ____. Mina tried to keep the lively baby dragons __ ____ __. They were all __ __ ____ __ __ ____ and keeping them still was a __ ____ __ __ __ __ __!

Use the text at the bottom of the page for dictation. The section for dictation can either be cut off by the teacher or be folded along the dotted line to allow the student to self-check their spellings on completion. Dictate the passage to the student. Ask her/him to spell the missing words, writing a sound on each line. Explain that longer lines indicate spellings with more than one letter, e.g. **p** **ark**.

The **f** **ar** **m** **er** had a plan to help them. He pointed to the back of his **c** **ar** **t**.

The **c** **ar** **t** was loaded with **b** **a** **s** **k** **e** **t** **s** of salt. They all hid in the back of the **c** **ar** **t** as the **f** **ar** **m** **er** drove the salt up to the **c** **a** **st** **le**. Mina tried to keep the lively baby dragons **c** **al** **m**. They were all **s** **t** **ar** **v** **i** **ng** and keeping them still was a **h** **ar** **d** **t** **a** **s** **k**!

Book 10: Breaking the Charm

Developing vocabulary: **cackled**

The word 'cackled' is used here in Book 10:

> 'cackled' means: laughed in a shrill, broken manner

Circle the word or phrase that could be replaced with the word 'cackled' in the following text:

> "The old lady in the play was really good," said Ben. "She was quite a nasty character and she laughed shrilly when she was talking."

Can you write two different sentences of your own using the word 'cackled'?

1.

____

____

2.

____

____

Book 10: Breaking the Charm

Reading fluency

The collector held up a large metal disc that sparkled in the light. He began to swing it to and fro. In a heartbeat it had started to charm them all! The baby dragons swayed sleepily. They were lost in a trance.

"I am the master of all your hearts!" cackled the collector, as his charm began to take hold.

Mina felt her heart pounding with fear. The trance was making her groggy. She stumbled into a vase and smashed it. A cloud of powder billowed right onto the face of the collector! He stumbled. The metal disc fell from his grasp.

The trance had been broken! Mina and Nat shook themselves. They quickly darted into a room next to the grand hall. A huge machine was in the middle of the room. At its heart was a sparkling scarlet gem.

Ask the student to read through the passage to familiarise themselves with the text.
Read it through for them again to model reading with expression and attention to punctuation.
Ask the student to read the passage again, thinking about adding expression to their reading and following punctuation in the passage. Students who struggle with punctuation may benefit from highlighting the punctuation in the text before reading.
Teachers can fold the page to cover the bottom paragraph of text to offer a shorter passage if needed.

Book 10: Breaking the Charm

Make a page for a comic – reading comprehension

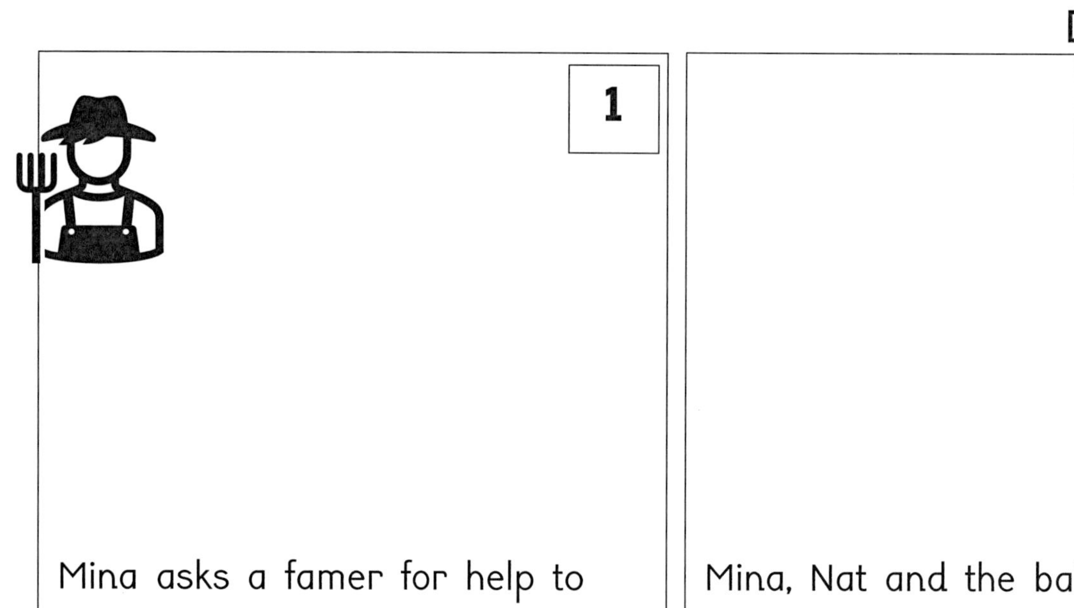

1

Mina asks a famer for help to find the last dragon egg. The farmer shows them the collector's castle. They realise the bounty hunters work for him!

2

Mina, Nat and the baby dragons smuggle into the castle in the back of the farmer's cart. They creep along the castle ramparts as it starts to get dark.

3

The collector appears and charms them all with a swinging disc! Mina and Nat escape and find a machine with the scarlet egg in the middle of it.

4

Nat rescues the final dragon egg. The group meet up with Bella in the starlit yard of the castle. Bella is so happy that her family have finally been reunited.

Ask the student to read the text and draw a picture to match the text in each box.

Book 10: Breaking the Charm

Dice game: words with 'ar' spellings

●	●●	●●●	●●●●	●●●●●	●●●●●●
past	harm	palm	laugh	mark	heart
mask	shark	alarm	starve	half	blast
aunt	craft	hearth	cart	park	path
calm	start	hearty	dance	dark	gasp
flask	spark	after	cars	carton	last

This game is for two players. Each player needs a batch of counters of one colour. The players take turns to throw the die. They read a word in the column that corresponds to the number on the die and place their counter on that word. The first to have three of her/his counters in a row in any direction is the winner.

Book 10: Breaking the Charm

Stepping stones reading game: 'ar' words

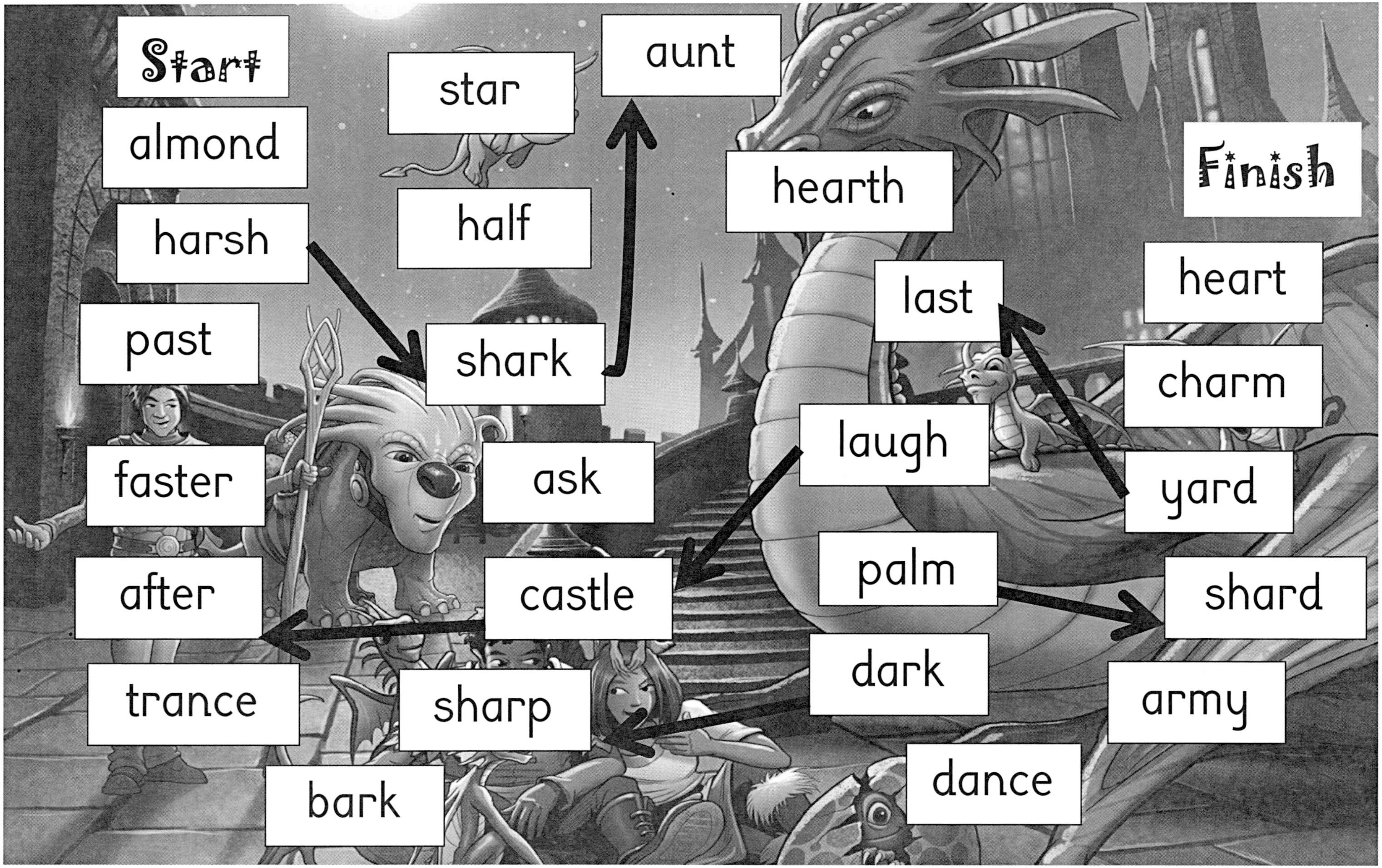

A game for 1–4 players: Play with counters and dice.

Players should read aloud the words that they land on at the end of each turn and follow the direction arrows if they land on them.

Book 10: Breaking the Charm

Spelling assessment: words with 'ar' spellings

1.

a	ar	al	ear	au
ask	car	palm	heart	laugh
fast	art	calm	hearth	draught
path	hard	half		

2.

a	ar	al
master	farmer	almond
father	shark	
plaster	alarm	

These lists can be used as a spelling assessment at the end of each book. The teacher can add words from list 2 for students who are ready for that stage. When dictating a word, first say the word on its own. Next, say a sentence with the word in it (to put the word in the context of a sentence) and then repeat the word. This ensures that the student has understood the word correctly, e.g. "Car. Mum had always wanted a red car. Car."

Appendix

Contents

* Pages 214, 215 and 216 are whole-page, printable certificates and charts and do not have page numbers.

Take home bookmark

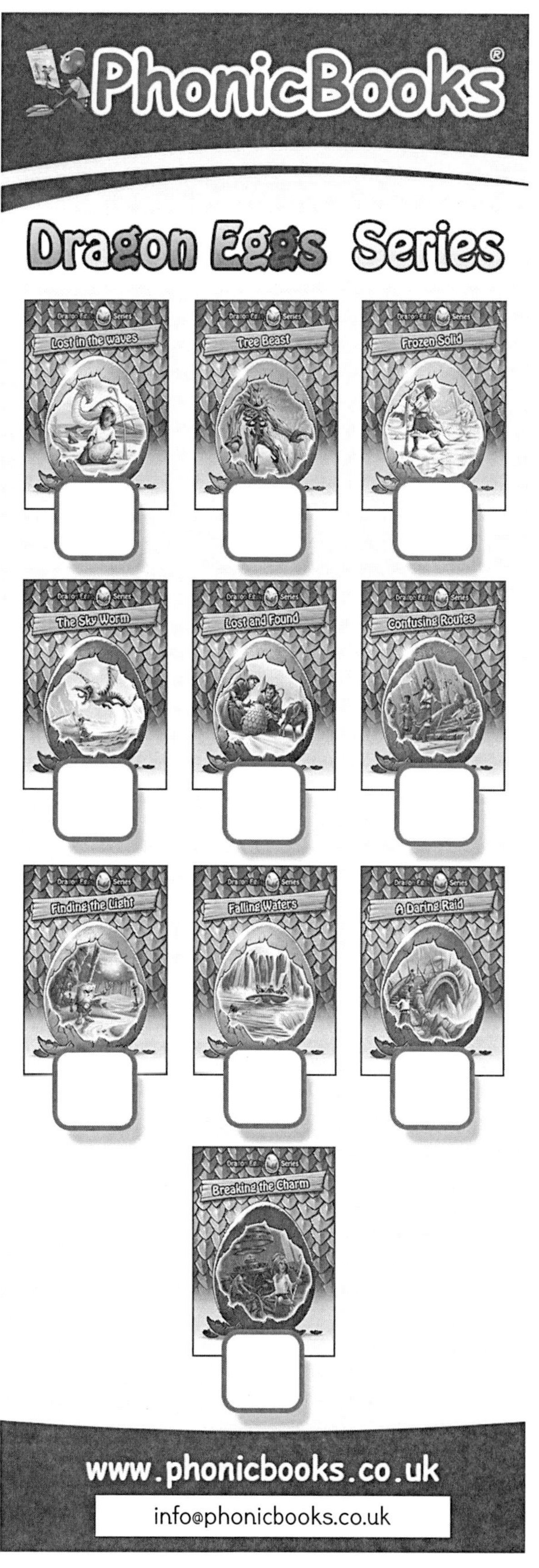

We have been working on the sound:

Help your child practise the different spellings of this sound using the reading practice page at the front of the book. Encourage them to blend the sounds together as they read the words.

This book has chapters, which allows for natural breaks when reading the book.

Have fun!

1. Enjoy reading this book with your child. If they have difficulties, share chapters or pages to relieve the reading strain.
2. If needed, model how to use punctuation and intonation to read with expression.
3. Encourage your child to read the book more than once as research shows that repeated reading of the same text helps to develop reading fluency. This can be done in a fun way by asking the reader to read the book to someone else or reading the book a second time with expression.

Choose which information box is most relevant and cut out and stick it to the reverse of the bookmark if sending home. Fill in the sound being worked on. The front of the bookmark can be used to identify the book currently being read or as a tick chart for the series.

Personal student bookmarks

Cut out for students to use as personal bookmarks. Tick or use stickers to record reading of each book in the series.

This sheet may be photocopied by the purchaser. © Phonic Books Ltd 2021

Dragon Eggs Series

Reading Certificate

Congratulations on completing a Dragon Eggs book!

____

Name

____

Book title

____

Teacher's signature

Dragon Eggs Series
tick chart

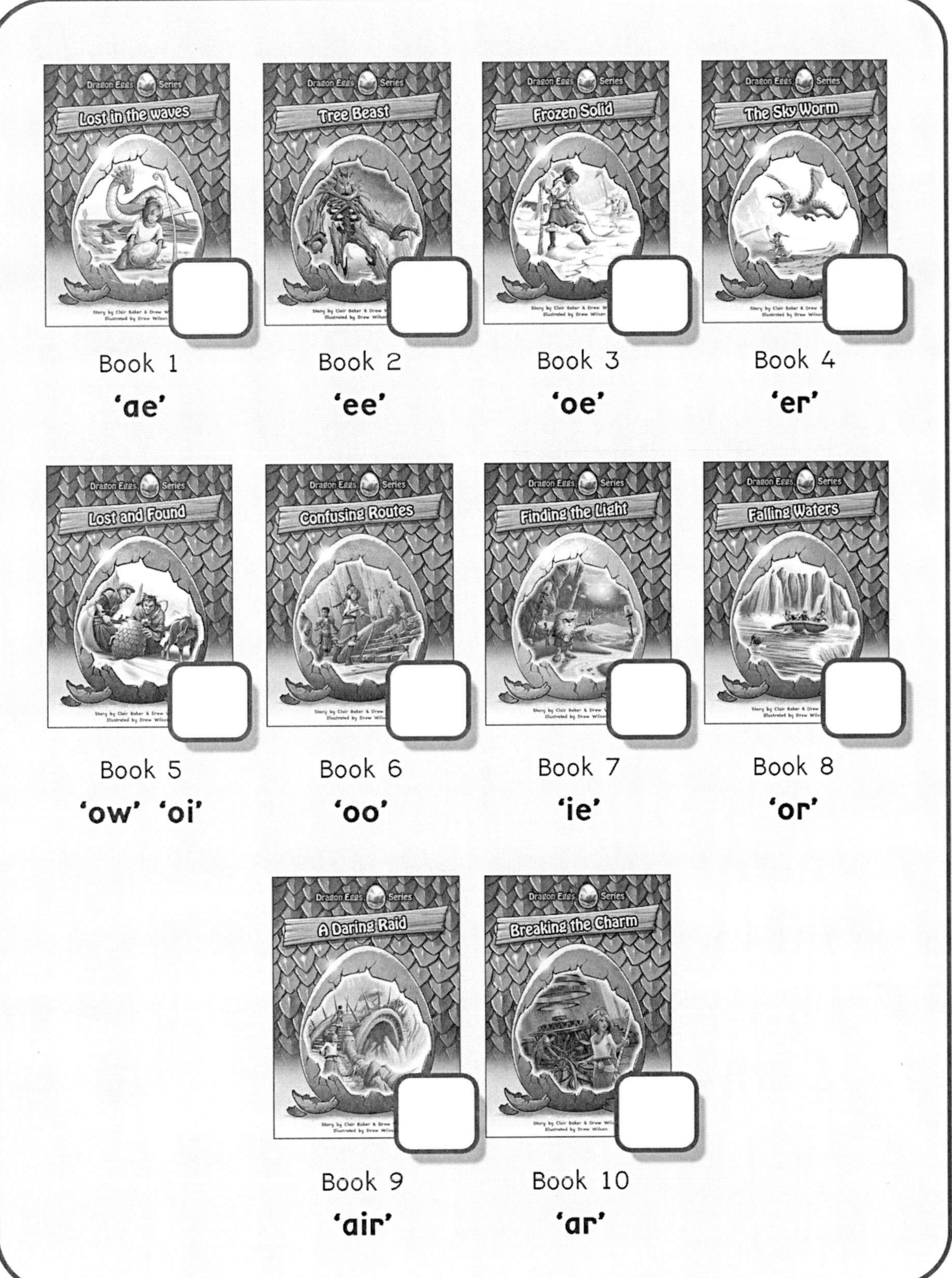

Dragon Eggs Series

Name

Teacher's signature

Congratulations on completing the whole Dragon Eggs Series!

Phonic Books®